MILLER'S
Classic
Motorcycles
PRICE GUIDE

MILLER'S CLASSIC MOTORCYCLES PRICE GUIDE 1995

Created and designed by
Miller's
The Cellars, High Street,
Tenterden, Kent, TN30 6BN
Tel: 01580 766411

Consultants: Judith & Martin Miller

General Editor: Valerie Lewis
Editorial and Production Co-ordinator: Sue Boyd
Editorial Assistants: Sue Montgomery, Marion Rickman, Jo Wood
Production Assistants: Helen Burt, Gillian Charles, Lorna Day
Advertising Executive: Melinda Williams
Advertising Assistant: Liz Warwick
Index compiled by: DD Editorial Services, Beccles
Design: Darren Manser, Jody Taylor, Stephen Parry

First published in Great Britain in 1994
by Miller's, an imprint of
Reed Consumer Books Limited,
Michelin House, 81 Fulham Road,
London SW3 6RB
and Auckland, Melbourne, Singapore and Toronto

© 1994 Reed International Books Limited

A CIP catalogue record for this book is
available from the British Library

ISBN 1-85732-541-9

Illustrations by Ashford Scanning Ltd.
Colour origination by Scantrans, Singapore
Printed and bound in England by William Clowes Ltd.,
Beccles and London

MILLER'S
Classic
Motorcycles
PRICE GUIDE

Consultants
Judith and Martin Miller

General Editor
Valerie Lewis

1995
Volume II

4

ACKNOWLEDGEMENTS

The publishers would like to acknowledge the great assistance given by our consultants.

Malcolm Barber   Sotheby's, 34-35 New Bond Street, London W1.

Jim Gleave   Atlantic Motorcycles, 20 Station Road, Twyford, Berks.

John Newson   Oxney Motorcycles, Rolvenden, Cranbrook, Kent

Jody Taylor   114 Pound Road, East Peckham, Tonbridge, Kent.

Brian Verrall   The Old Garage, High Street, Handcross, Haywards Heath, West Sussex

Mick Walker   10 Barton Road, Wisbech, Cambs.

KEY TO ILLUSTRATIONS

Each illustration and descriptive caption is accompanied by a letter code. By referring to the following list of Auctioneers (denoted by *), Dealers (•) and Clubs (‡), the source of any item may be immediately determined. Inclusion in this edition in no way constitutes or implies a contract or binding offer on the part of any of our contributors to supply or sell the goods illustrated, or similar articles, at the prices stated. Advertisers in this year's directory are denoted by †.

ACC • Albert's, 113 London Road, Twickenham, Middx. Tel: 0181 891 3067

AT • Andrew Tiernan Vintage & Classic Motorcycles, Old Railway Station, Station Road, Framlingham, Woodbridge, Suffolk. Tel: 01728 724321

AtMC •† Atlantic Motor Cycles, 20 Station Road, Twyford, Berkshire. Tel: 01734 342266

BCA • Beaulieu Cars Automobilia, Beaulieu, Hants. Tel: 01590 612689

BCB • Bristol Classic Bikes, 17 Church Road, Redfield, Bristol. Tel: 0117 955 7762

BKS * Robert Brooks (Auctioneers) Ltd., 81 Westside, London SW4. Tel: 0171-228 8000

Bro • John Brown, Letchworth, Herts. Tel: 01462 682589

CBr •† Cooper Bros. Classic Motorcycles, Shipston-on-Stour, Nr Stratford-upon-Avon, Warwicks. Tel: 01789 267100

CCR •† Charnwood Classic Restorations, 107, Central Road, Hugglescote, Coalville, Leicester. Tel: 01530 832357

COYS * Coys of Kensington, 2/4 Queens Gate Mews, London SW7. Tel: 0171 584 7444

CRMC ‡ Classic Racing Motorcycle Club, c/o Simon Wilson, 6 Pendennis Road, Freshbrook, Swindon, Wilts. Tel: 01793 610828

CStC • Cake Street Classics, Bellview, Cake Street, Laxfield, Nr Woodbridge, Suffolk. Tel: 01986 798504

DDM * Dickinson, Davy & Markham, Wrawby Street, Brigg, S. Humberside. Tel: 01652 653666

EM • Essex Motorsports International Inc., 244 Middlesex Turnpike, Chester, Connecticut 06412, USA. Tel: (0101) 203 526 2060

FHF •† Foulkes-Halbard of Filching, Filching Manor, Jevington Road, Wannock, Polegate, Sussex. Tel: 01323 487838/487124

GLC •† Greenlooms Classics, Greenlooms Farm, Hargrave, Chester. Tel: 01829 781636

HC • Heritage Classics. Tel: 01206 211954

HH •† Hughie Hancox Restorations, rear of O'Briens Buildings, 203-269 Foleshill Road, Coventry. Tel: 01203 552305

HM • Harris Motorcycles. Tel: 01622 675404

HOLL * Holloways, 49 Parsons Street, Banbury, Oxon. Tel: 01295 253197

LF * Lambert & Foster, 77 Commercial Road, Paddock Wood, Kent. Tel: 01892 832325

LW * Lawrences Auctioneers, Norfolk House, 80 High Street, Bletchingley, Surrey. Tel: 01883 743323

MCh •† Michael Chapman. Tel: 01789 773897

MMC • Mason Motorcycles, Fountain Road, Barn Street, Haverfordwest, Dyfed. Tel: 01437 765651

MR *† Martyn Rowe, The Truro Auction Centre, Calenick Street, Truro, Cornwall. Tel: 01872 260020

MVT ‡ Military Vehicle Trust, PO Box 6, Fleet, Hants

ONS * Onslows, Metrostore, Townmead Road, London SW6. Tel: 0171 793 0240

OxM •† Oxney Motorcycles, Rolvenden, Cranbrook, Kent. Tel: 01797 270119

PC Private Collection.

PM • Pollard's Motorcycles, The Garage, Clarence Street, Dinnington, Nr Sheffield. Tel: 01909 563310

PMB •† Pooks Motor Bookshop, Fowke Street, Rothley, Leics. Tel: 0116 237 6222

PS * Palmer Snell, 65 Cheap Street, Sherbourne, Dorset. Tel: 01935 812218

RCMC •† Robertsbridge Classic Motorcycles, Western House, Station Road, Robertsbridge, East Sussex. Tel: 01580 880323

RJES • Robin James Engineering Services, Clinton Road, Leominster, Herefordshire. Tel: 01568 612800

RSk •† Rob Skipsey Scooters. Tel: 01430 440057/01836 544059

S *† Sotheby's, 34-35 New Bond Street, London W1. Tel: 0171 493 8080.

VER •† Brian Verrall, The Old Garage, High St, Handcross, Haywards Heath, West Sussex. Tel: 01444 400678

WCM •† Wilson Classic Motorcycles, PO Box 88, Crewe. Tel: 01270 668523

CONTENTS

HOW TO USE THIS BOOK

Miller's Classic Motorcycles Price Guide presents an overview of the classic motorcycle marketplace during the past twelve months. In order to give you a comprehensive feel for what is available, we have included illustrations from a wide range of auction houses, dealers, motorcycle clubs and private individuals.

Following Miller's format, motorcycles are presented alphabetically by marque and chronologically within each group. Sidecars, specials, mopeds and scooters are dealt with in the same way at the end of the book. In the motorcycle memorabilia section, objects are grouped alphabetically by type, for example clothing and ephemera, and then, where possible, chronologically within each grouping. Each illustration is fully captioned and carries a price range which reflects the dealer's/auctioneer's sale price. The prefix 'Est.' indicates the estimated price for the motorcycles which remained unsold at auction. Each illustration also carries an identification code which enables the reader to locate its source in the Key to Illustrations.

We do not illustrate every classic motorcycle ever produced. Our aim is to reflect the market place, so if, for example, there appears to be a large number of Triumphs and only a few Vincents, this is a reflection of the quantity, availability and, to an extent, the desirability of these motorcycles in the marketplace over the last twelve months. If the motorcycle you are looking for is not featured under its alphabetical listing, do look in the colour sections and double-check the index. If a particular motorcycle is not featured this year, it may well have appeared in the previous edition of *Miller's Classic Motorcycle Price Guide,* which provides a growing visual reference library.

Please remember Miller's pricing policy: we provide you with a price GUIDE and not a price LIST. Our price ranges, worked out by a team of trade and auction house experts, reflect variables such as condition, location, desirability, and so on. Don't forget that if you are selling, it is possible that you will be offered less than the price range.

Lastly, we are always keen to improve the content and accuracy of our guides. If you feel that a particular make or model or other aspect of classic motorcycles has not been covered in sufficient detail, or if you have any other comments you would like to share with us about our book, please write and let us know. We value feedback from the people who use this guide to tell us how we can make it even better for them.

STATE OF THE MARKET

The trend towards an enthusiast-led market which first became evident in 1992–3 has continued, with the United Kingdom market in particular becoming broader-based. A number of factors have influenced this, not the least of which is the establishment of a true free market in Europe from January 1993 onwards. The fact that our European partners can now buy motorcycles in the UK – and, indeed, sell them too – without the imposition of VAT when borders are crossed, means that many more overseas enthusiasts have been present at auctions and, particularly where exchange rates have been favourable, bidding strongly.

The gradual strengthening of the American economy, and the value of the dollar exchange rate has meant a return to UK markets of American buyers following an absence of several years, and this too has had its effect. With an increase in overseas buying, a strong defensive home market is also created, but whilst this has tended to increase the number of buyers at sales, it has not materially affected prices except at the top of the market.

There are a number of reasons for this, one being that between 1990 and 1993 – rather like the housing market – there were more motorcycles for sale than there were buyers. This backlog of unsold machines dictates that we are still to a large degree experiencing a buyer's market. Plenty of machines are on offer, which has kept prices reasonable, and although these are beginning to rise now, the graph is rising at a shallow angle making it an excellent time to buy.

Variety continues to be good, with more and more early Japanese machines now being collectable. This is due to the Vintage Motor Cycle Club's rolling-on 25 year rule. Japanese machines are now becoming eligible for the Club's activities and membership, and there is also sufficient interest to support a separate Vintage Japanese Motorcycle Club. Standards of restoration are improving all the time, and it is encouraging to see these being applied to Japanese machines.

During the period when the American dollar was low against the pound many machines were imported from the US. Some of these were indigenous makes like Indian and Harley-Davidson, whilst others were variants of British-made models which had been made specifically for the US market. Some of these had never been seen before in Britain, and their emergence now, following restoration, has added greatly to the volume and variety of bikes on offer.

Japan has once again emerged as a strong buying area, despite the decline in the Japanese economy but, as before, their interest is mainly confined to quality machines like Vincents, Brough-Superiors,

BSA Gold Stars and other erstwhile high flyers. Many machines appear to be destined for museums established by the Japanese motor manufacturers themselves. We have also seen well-restored examples of Japanese classics returning to the land of their origin.

In the four years which followed the onset of the recession, motorcycle dealers generally had a hard time, and many of them succumbed. Those which survived tended to be either the longer-established dealers who had seen it all before, or those who had resisted the temptation to overstock with expensive machines on a rising market at the end of the eighties, using borrowed money. As a result, the surviving motorcycle trade is a leaner, fitter beast, and it is encouraging to see active dealer participation at auction.

There is a trend, however, for dealers today to hold smaller stocks, and to establish markets before buying. One prominent Yorkshire dealer has been making regular trips to Japan, and has obviously established an outlet there. Other dealers are selling machines on 'sale or return' and we have also seen several well-known dealers buying 'on commission' – in other words, buying on behalf of a private client who prefers to remain anonymous.

Most buyers outside the trade, are enthusiasts rather than investors, and therefore are more knowledgeable. Also because there is such an enormous choice at the moment, they are far more discriminate than in the past. Buyers will view several machines before deciding which to buy. Green shoots there most definitely are, although some dealers feel that some of their colleagues in the trade are prone to exaggerate the level of business they are doing.

As always, exceptional machines make exceptional money, and the Sotheby's Classic Bike Auction at the RAF Museum, Hendon, provided the forum for some record prices. The 1947/53 Vincent 'Nero', estimated at £30,000–32,000, soared to a new record of £55,400 and went to the National Motorcycle Museum.

Flat tank vintage and pioneer machines are currently enjoying a resurgence of interest, and barn discoveries – particularly those with interesting histories – continue to attract top prices in original condition. The 1921 BSA combination sold at Hendon had only had one owner since 1925 and made £6,095 against a pre-sale estimate of £3,000–4,000. As before, British singles and twins of the 1940s, 50s and 60s continue to dominate the market, with better Japanese classics now in evidence.

Malcolm Barber
Sotheby's – Senior Director

IMPORTING OR EXPORTING
CLASSIC MOTORCYCLES

The rules governing the importation of any motor vehicle into the UK are complicated, but those covering motorcycles need to be carefully examined as they do not always follow those affecting private cars. If a classic motorcycle is imported into the UK from outside the EC, there are a number of categories into which it can fall, and these may be summarised as follows:

Motorcycles built in the EC but exported new to a non-EC country

Normally a machine exported new would not pay VAT in the country of origin and if it returns either to that country or another EC member country, then VAT would be payable, but not Duty.

Motorcycles built in the UK after August 1940 and exported new to a non-EC country

Purchase tax was introduced in the UK in August 1940 as a 'temporary wartime measure'. Its successor, VAT, is still with us. A machine bought after the introduction of purchase tax would have been liable to that tax, unless it was exported. If it subsequently returned now, VAT would have to be paid.

Motorcycles built in the UK before August 1940 and exported new to a non-EC country

Regardless of whether a motorcycle was made before August 1940 and then exported, it would be liable for VAT (but not Duty) upon its subsequent return to the UK, unless it could obtain exemption under the 'historic' designation under tariff heading 97.05.

Machines previously in free circulation in an EC country

Provided proof could be produced of previous free circulation status, then no VAT or Duty would be payable upon that machine's return to the EC or UK. Machines would be classified as British Returned Goods if they had been previously in free circulation in the UK, but there are some qualifying conditions:
1. They must not have been exported outside the EC for process or repair.
2. Proof must be provided of the date of manufacture or previous free circulation status.
3. Goods have to be returned within three years of their export, although there is provision for this requirement to be waived, under declaration CPC 40 09 58.
Evidence of previous free circulation would include a statement from the DVLA confirming that the vehicle had been registered in a permanent tax paid registration series prior to export, or a statement confirming free circulation status from the vehicle's manufacturer or the Registrar of the Owner's Club, or the production of registration

documents matching the frame and engine numbers of the machine. Information would also be accepted from a motor museum, or a body or individual recognised as being a competent authority by HM Customs & Excise.

Motorcycles qualifying for 'historical' status under tariff heading 97.05

The blanket agreement to treat cars as 'historic' over a certain age does not apply to motorcycles, and regardless of their age and antiquity a case has to be made for them if they are to be considered as 'historic' by HM Customs & Excise and qualifying for tariff heading 97.05. A tricycle, three-wheeled car, or motorcycle combination is a car rather than a motorcycle, and therefore subject to the blanket agreement, whereas a two-wheeled motorcycle is not.

There are a number of different categories under which HM Customs & Excise might agree that a motorcycle was 'historic', but it is by no means a foregone conclusion that a machine will be accepted. Each case is considered on its merits.
1. A machine of extreme antiquity.
2. A machine which by virtue of its technical specification and age represents a 'milestone in development' of the motorcycle.
3. A machine associated with a famous event.
4. A machine associated with a famous person.
5. A prototype.

It is important that if a machine is given an 'historic' classification under tariff heading 97.05, it is automatically exempt from both Duty and,by virtue of the appropriate VAT Special Provisions Order, from VAT. Generally speaking, it is desirable that any approach to HM Customs & Excise for 'historic' status on a machine should be made by a body or individual recognised by them as being competent to adjudicate on such matters, as the chances of success are far higher.

Importation from within the EC

From 1st January 1993, New Means of Transport (NMT) are liable for VAT in the destination state when they are supplied in one EC Member State for removal to another. In the case of cars and motorcycles, according to HM Customs VAT Control Division in Liverpool, an NMT is either less than three months old, or has travelled under its own power for no more than 3,000 kilometres. Any motorcycle which is not an NMT by this designation, and which is VAT paid within the EC, is allowed from circulation and would not be liable to VAT or Duty upon entry to the UK. However, certain countries within the EC have instituted VRT (Vehicle Registration Tax) on imported vehicles, and these include Ireland, Belgium, Germany and Denmark. Fortunately the UK has not, as yet, introduced this additional tax.

11

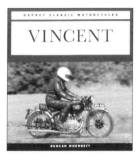
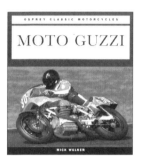
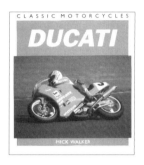
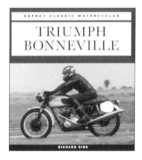

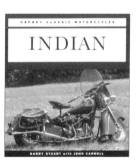

ABC *(British)*

ABC – All British (Engine) Company – was established in 1913, and the following year was reorganised and named ABC Motors Ltd., which specialised in motorcycle engines for the military. It was not until 1919 that Sopwith-ABC began to design and build motorcycles, commencing with the transverse-mounted 398cc flat twin which was the predecessor of the first BMW. In 1921 Sopwith went into liquidation. However, between 1920–1924 ABCs, which included the 348cc and 493cc, continued to be made in France under licence from Sopwith.

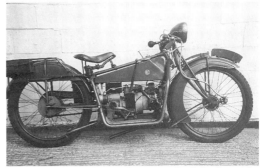

1921 ABC Flat Twin 400cc, built by Sopwith Aviation Co. of Brooklands, designed by Granville Bradshaw.
£5,000–£5,500 *AT*

This machine has been featured in British Bike Magazine *and has been displayed in the Brooklands Museum for the past four years.*

1921 ABC Overhead Valve Twin 350cc.
£3,500–4,000 *VER*

AJS *(British)*

The first AJS was built in 1909 by the Stevens Brothers at Wolverhampton. By 1927 they had introduced racing engines with chain-driven ohc in 348cc and 498cc versions. In 1931 AJS was sold to Matchless and moved to London. For many years following the merger, although the two bikes had many parts in common, the AJS marque remained a separate entity.

1924 AJS Model BI 2¾hp 348cc, flat tank, period lighting, very good condition.
£3,500–4,000 *S*

AERMACCHI *(Italian)*

1964 Aermacchi Ala D'oro 250cc Solo Racer, finished in Italian racing red, excellent condition mechanically.
£4,400–4,800 *S*

This bike's competition history is well documented by contemporary race reports.

1925 AJS Big Port 350cc.
£6,500–7,000 *AtMC*

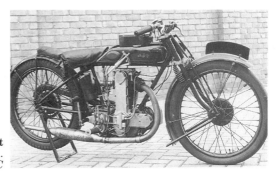

c1927 AJS Model 7R Overhead Camshaft 350cc, very rare racing model.
£8,250–8,500 *AtMC*

1930 AJS Model R6 348cc, overhead valve engine,
4 speed hand change gear, black paintwork, very
good original upholstery, carbide lamps fitted from
new, excellent condition throughout, spare parts,
original tools, manuals and tyre pump, with
old logbook.
Est. £4,500–5,000 *S*

*The original owner's name and address appear in
the service books.*

**1931 AJS S12 Overhead Valve Single Cylinder
248cc Sports Model,** matching frame and
engine numbers.
£1,700–2,000 *PS*

*One of the last of the original AJS models to be made
in the Stevens Brothers' factory in Wolverhampton.
Used extensively in vintage motorcycle events during
the seventies.*

1938 AJS Twin Port 350cc.
£4,500–5,000 *AtMC*

1930 AJS R4 350cc, single side valve engine,
3 speed gearbox, restored, good mechanical
order, very good cosmetically.
Est. £2,600–2,800 *S*

1936 AJS 36/7R 350cc, fitted with a Burman racing
gearbox and kickstart, rebuilt to a very high
standard, full lighting set and rubber Dunlop
saddle, some 1937 features.
£10,400–10,600 *S*

*This fine example of a 'cammy' AJS was possibly
supplied to the company's works rider, Harold
Daniels, for the 1937 season. However, due to his
move to the competition at Bracebridge Street, it was
never actively campaigned by him. This honour fell
to John Hudson who purchased the machine in 1938
from Jack Daniels for the sum of £37.10s.0d.*

1950 AJS 7R 350cc Racing, finished in black and
gold, original specification, candlestick rear
suspension units.
Est. £11,500–12,000 *S*

- **7Rs are highly noted for their racing
  achievements both in the past and in
  contemporary classic events.**
- **AJS merged with Matchless in 1937 to
  form AMC.**
- **In 1956 only, 'Jampots' became a
  feature of the 600cc AJS 30.**

1953 AJS 18S 500cc, finished in black, good
original condition, and good mechanically.
Est. £1,000–2,000 *LF*

1955 AJS 350cc Trials Replica, based on a G3L Trials motorcycle.
£900–1,100 *MR*

1956 AJS G80 Overhead Valve 500cc, American import, Jampot rear suspension.
£2,000–2,650 *CBr*

1956 AJS 30 600cc, traditional black with chromium plated front panels, thoroughly restored throughout, only one owner.
Est. £2,000–2,500 *S*

A fine example of one of the scarcer twin cylinder models.

1956 AJS Model 18 500cc.
£2,500–2,600 *WCM*

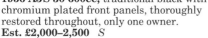

1957 AJS International 500cc.
£3,250–3,500 *CBr*

1958 AJS 350cc Trials, black paintwork and upholstery, very good condition.
£4,600–5,000 *S*

This trials bike is eligible for pre-65 trials

1964 AJS Model 14 250cc, complete and original condition, engine requires restoration.
Est. £400–500 *S*

1964 AJS 33 CSR 750cc, 17,000 miles from new, excellent original condition.
£3,250–3,500 *S*

A fine example of a scarcer large capacity twin.

ANSEL

Ansel 350cc Grass Track, 5 stud JAP engine and Norton gearbox converted to 2 speeds, BTH racing magneto, excellent metallic blue frame, white mudguards.
Est. £1,000–1,200 *S*

ANTIG

1961 Antig 500cc Grass Track Racing, 1948 4 stud JAP engine, 2 speed Norton gearbox, painted blue, very good condition throughout
Est. £1,200–1,300 *S*

ARIEL *(British)*

Although Ariel was building three-wheelers in 1898 it was not until 1902 that they began to build motorcycles. Beginning first with a 3.5hp single cylinder, by WWI Ariel had expanded their range to include 498cc sv singles and 998cc ioe V-twins. After WWII Ariel production focused on the popular 347cc and 497cc ohv Red Hunter singles and competition motorcycles. During the late 1950s, Jack Sangster, the owner of Ariel and also head of BSA, moved Ariel into the BSA factory at Birmingham. There the famous 247cc vertical twin 2 strokes, the Leader and the Arrow, were designed. However, the 197cc version was to be the last Ariel model created and the marque ceased production in 1970.

1930 Ariel Touring 550cc, restoration project, requires parts to complete.
£900–1,000 *S*

1938 Ariel Red Hunter 350cc.
£2,500–3,250 *PM*

This bike was noted for it's unusual bright red colour at a time when most bikes were painted black with gold lines. It was extremely popular before WWII and was also successful in motocross and trials.

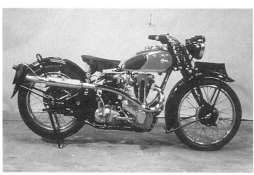

1936 Ariel Red Hunter 250cc, restored to an exceptional standard throughout with no known deviations from catalogue specification.
£3,700–4,000 *S*

1939 Ariel Square Four Model H9 1000cc, excellent condition throughout, with correct silencers.
£5,000–5,500 *S*

Designed by Edward Turner in 1930, the Ariel Square Four proved to be one of the longest-lived of all classic motorcycles. Until 1958 it was offered in both overhead valve and overhead camshaft guise in 500cc, 600cc and 1000cc sizes

1943 Ariel Model XG 350cc, overhead valve single cylinder engine, black and silver livery, girder forks with coil spring suspension and rigid rear frame.
£1,800–2,000 *S*

This motorcycle is believed to have originally been a military machine.

1947 Ariel Red Hunter 350cc, Anstey link rear suspension and telescopic front forks, finished in black, good original condition.
£1,900–2,100 *S*

1948 Ariel Red Hunter 350cc, finished with correct red painted tank and wheel lining, black frame and mudguards, restored to high standard throughout, optional pillion seat and footrests.
£1,500–1,800 *S*

1949 Ariel Square Four 1000cc, 4 cylinder engine, completely restored.
£3,200–3,500 *BCB*

1952 Ariel Square Four 995cc, alloy engine and coil ignition first introduced in 1949, very good condition throughout.
Est. £2,600–2,800 *S*

Miller's is a price GUIDE not a price LIST

1951 Ariel Red Hunter 500cc.
£2,500–3,000 *WCM*

1955 Ariel Red Hunter 350cc, restored.
£1,500–1,850 *BCB*

1955 Ariel Square Four Solo 997cc, finished in black to very high standard, mechanically sound, combining features of the MKI and MKII models.
£3,500–4,000 *S*

c1956 Ariel Colt 198cc, very good condition throughout.
Est. £800–900 *S*

1956 Ariel Red Hunter 500cc, good running order, old style log book.
£1,900–2,100 *S*

1956 Ariel Square Four Solo 997cc, finished in traditional maroon, sound mechanical condition throughout, extensive rebuild, including alloy rims, stainless steel fittings and battery box.
£4,250–4,500 *S*

1957 Ariel Scrambler 350cc, rebuilt condition with new tyres, alloy mud-guards and petrol tank.
Est. £4,000–4,200 *S*

This motorcycle was believed to have been built by the factory as a prototype for evaluation purposes in the hands of Gordon Blakeway, before being restored and sold by the factory in 1959.

- **The 200cc Colt first appeared in 1953 drawing heavily on BSA parts for its creation.**
- **The Ariel Square Four offered high maximum speed and good acceleration while link rear suspension and a sprung saddle ensured rider comfort.**
- **Coil ignition was first introduced in 1949.**

1958 Ariel Red Hunter.
£3,250–3,500 *AtMC*

1963 Ariel 500cc, Rickman frame, late type Cerani forks, running condition.
£1,250–1,500 *CBr*

1966 Ariel Pixie 49cc Overhead Valve Single Cylinder Model, completely overhauled and in very good condition, original green registration book.
£320–360 *PS*

This small capacity machine was made by Ariel in an unsuccessful attempt to break into the moped market.

BARTON (British)

c1977 Barton 750cc Racing, restoration project.
£250–300 *S*

The Barton concern met with considerable success during the late 1970s and early 1980s with their Suzuki derived engines and Spondon framed machines.

BMW (German)

Production of Bayerische Motoren Werke (BMW) motorcycles began in Munich in 1921, but is now carried out at Spandau. Noted in the early days for its horizontally opposed twin cylinder engine with its semi-unit construction layout and shaft drive, this basic design still exists today alongside the K-series three and four cylinder models. From 1928–1950 BMW produced supercharged machines for several famous works riders. When Germany became a member of the FIM, superchargers were no longer allowed.

1951 BMW R51/3 494cc, fully restored throughout, in excellent condition.
£2,400–2,800 *S*

1959 BMW R60.
£4,250–4,500 *AtMC*

1955 BMW R50, fully restored.
£3,800–4,000 *MMC*

BENELLI (Italian)

c1970 Benelli Tornado 650cc Solo, finished in red with white striping, with chromium mudguards, in good running order.
£450–550 *S*

Benelli's 105mph Tornado Twin was developed primarily for sale in the United States and is consequently rarely seen on this side of the Atlantic. It handled well and perhaps deserved to meet with greater success. However, it was competing against a number of well established twins, most notably those from Norton and Triumph.

1975 Benelli 2C 250cc, good mechanical and cosmetic condition, rebuilt.
£400–500 *S*

Following the de Tomaso takeover of Benelli, a complete revision of the company's products was initiated which resulted in a product line that was aimed at their Japanese competitors, amongst which were two 2 stroke twins, a 124.7cc model, and the 231.4cc 2C. Whilst its performance was on a par with its competitors, with typically fine Italian handling qualities, its 6 volt electrical system and pre-mix lubrication did not help sales.

1959 BMW R60 600cc, very good original condition, with manufacturer's instruction manual, first registered on 9th June, 1961.
Est. £2,800–3,200 *S*

1960 BMW R26 250cc.
£1,250–1,500 *PM*

1965 BMW R60 594cc Horizontally Opposed Twin Cylinder Model, in good original condition, fitted with stainless steel exhaust pipes, original tool kit, buff log book.
£1,250–1,500 *PS*

BOWN *(British)*

c1950 Bown Autocycle.
£100–150 *LF*

BROUGH-SUPERIOR *(British)*

George Brough spared no expense when he built the Brough-Superior motorcycle. As a result they are known today as the 'Rolls-Royce' among motorcycles. Some of the most famous models included the SS100 ohv and SS8 sv V-twins.
After WWII, Brough could not find suitable engines to warrant continuing production.

1927 Brough-Superior SS100.
£20,000–25,000 *LF*

1925 Brough-Superior SS100.
£35,000+ *AtMC*

c1928 Brough-Superior Pendine SS100.
£35,000+ *AtMC*

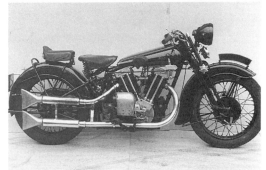

1930 Brough-Superior 680cc Solo, finished in black with gold lining, good condition throughout.
£12,500–13,000 *S*
This example of the baby overhead valve Brough was despatched from the works on 6th June, 1930 and according to the factory record card, was originally fitted with a Cruiser sidecar.

1930 Brough-Superior 680 Overhead Valve.
£12,500–12,850 *VER*

BSA *(British)*

Birmingham Small Arms (BSA) started life in 1906 as a supplier of cycle parts to British and foreign factories. It was not long afterwards that they began to produce motorised bicycles and then motorcycles. By 1921 their first sv V-twin 770cc was built and successfully marketed. This led to an extensive range of models – which included versions of ohv, sv, round tanks, singles and 2 strokes which could be supplied with vertical or inclined engines – produced throughout the 1920s and 30s. After WWII the Gold Star became one of the most popular sports machines built in England. Yet despite the introduction of several new models and having once held the title of being England's leading motorcycle manufacturer, BSA ceased production in 1971. The company was reconstructed in the late 1970s to produce lightweights for export and replica Manx Norton frames.

1938 Brough Superior SS100 1000cc Overhead Valve.
£19,000–20,000 *VER*

- BSA's sidevalve singles offered a combination of good performance, high build quality at a reasonable cost.
- It was machines such as the B series that enabled BSA to survive the depression years of the 30s, by offering cheap reliable transport.
- Threatened by Triumph's Speed Twin and Tiger 100, BCA released the 500 A7 twin in 1949.
- Gold Star machines of all types are now eagerly sought after by collectors, but the competition versions are rarer.

1914 BSA 4hp, belt drive, good condition.
£3,000–4,500 *AT*
This was BSA's third year of motorcycle production, and their early bikes were built on the principles of gun manufacturing with every part numbered and hand-finished.

1922 BSA 557cc Tourer, excellent overall condition with full alloy chaincase, full acetylene lighting kit, period horn and leather-fronted tool boxes mounted on the rear carrier.
£3,000–3,500 *S*

1923 BSA 500 Sports, 493cc, traditionally finished in green and black with cream trim, fitted with rear luggage carrier and period horn.
£3,300–3,800 *S*

1924 BSA 250cc 'Round Tank', finished in traditional livery with correct transfers and Lucas acetylene front lamp, Raydyot tower rear lamp, luggage carrier and a tyre pump.
£2,800–3,200 *S*

1927 BSA 2.5hp 249cc De Luxe Single Cylinder Side Valve Model, good running order, good all-round condition, fitted with modern twistgrip and a later carburettor.
£1,900–2,100 *PS*

1928 BSA L28SS 350cc Overhead Valve Single, an unrestored vintage machine.
£1,250–1,750 *RCMC*

Based on the BSA model that performed so well in the 1926 ISDT, this machine was ridden in the Isle of Man TT Rally several years ago by a well-known clubman. A very interesting and genuine vintage motorcycle, originally owned by the Debenham sisters, Nancy and Betty, who rode in BSA competitions.

1929 BSA 500cc Sloper.
£2,500–3,000 *AtMC*

1928 BSA 500cc Sloper.
Est. £900–1,200 *S*

Affectionately known as the 'Sloper', because of the inclination of the engine.

1934 BSA B150 148cc, original condition.
£850–1,000 *S*

1934 BSA B2 250cc Overhead Valve.
£850–1,000 *AT*

1934 BSA Blue Star 350cc.
£4,250–4,500 *AtMC*

1937 BSA Y13 750cc Overhead Valve V-Twin,
very good conditon.
£9,000–10,000 *AT*

This is one of the finest pre-war BSA's – a much under-rated machine.

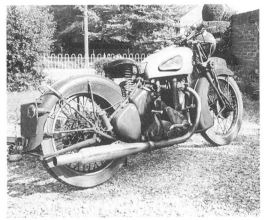

1938 (1939 registered) BSA Silver Star 500cc
Single, in need of restoration.
£1,200–1,500 *HOLL*

1938 BSA M20 500cc, originally in military
service, rebuilt to civilian specification, good
all-round condition.
£1,600–2,000 *S*

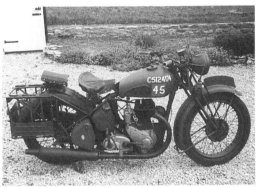

1943 BSA M20 500cc Side valve.
£1,400–1,600 *MVT*

Almost every WWII despatch rider rode one of these bikes at some stage in his career.

c1944 BSA M20.
£1,000–1,200 *MVT*

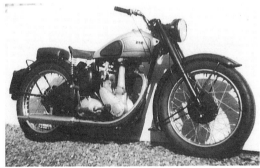

1946 BSA B31 350cc, restored,
good running condition.
£1,250–1,450 *CStC*

1948 BSA A7 500cc.
£2,400–2,600 *WCM*

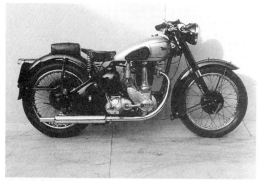

1949 BSA B33 500cc.
£2,750–3,000 *VER*

1949 BSA B31 350cc.
£2,250–2,500 *AtMC*

1949 BSA B31 350cc.
£2,000–2,500 *WCM*

c1950 BSA M21 600cc Side Valve, rigid frame
with telescopic forks, original condition.
£580–600 *MR*

1950 BSA A7 Star Twin, only one owner,
original registration number, fully restored,
replacement carburettors.
Est. £2,100–2,300 *S*

1950 BSA C10 250cc Side Valve Special,
good condition.
£1,300–1,600 *RCMC*

1951 BSA ZB34A 500cc Pre-Unit Single,
good condition.
£2,500–3,500 *RCMC*

*This competition model is wrongly called by some
a 'Gold Star'. It is a 500cc alloy barrelled model for
trials, scrambling or racing, imported from the
States and put into road trim.*

1951 BSA Bantam D1 125cc, rigid rear frame,
restored to original specification throughout.
£1,200–1,400 *S*

*This bike has taken highly commended awards at
many Custom and Classic shows.*

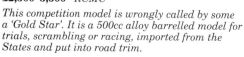

1951 BSA Bantam D1 125cc,
good original condition.
£600–900 *RCMC*

1952 BSA Gold Star ZB32 348cc, restored,
original apart from 80mph Smith's speedometer
instead of 120mph instrument, and an Amal
Monobloc, originally with a rigid rear end.
£2,900–3,100 *S*

1952 BSA B31 350cc, original condition.
£1,450–1,750 *BCB*

1953 BSA A7 500cc, twin cylinder overhead
valve engine, good condition throughout,
paintwork fair, original maker's specification,
old style green log book.
£1,300–1,500 *S*

c1953 BSA BB34 GS Trials, 500cc
single cylinder engine, in good condition
throughout, no known alterations from
maker's original specification.
£2,200–2,500 *S*

1953 BSA B31 350cc, maroon, rare plunger model,
restored to original specification.
Est. £1,500–2,000 *HOLL*

> ### Did you know?
> **MILLER'S Collectors
> Classic Motorcycles Price
> Guide** *builds up year-by-
> year to form the most
> comprehensive photo
> library system available.*

1953 BSA C10 250cc, finished in red,
excellent cosmetic condition and good
running order.
Est. £600–700 *S*

1953 BSA Gold Star CB32 350cc Racer,
fully restored throughout.
£5,000–6,000 *S*

*This bike was ridden by Fred Wallis in the
Junior Clubman's TT on the Isle of Man in
1954, knocking some five seconds off the lap
record on his first outing before regrettably
crashing at Laurel Bank. Wallis continued to
campaign CB32 627 and at Aberdare in 1958
was to finish ahead of Phil Read at one
meeting, and Norton-mounted Mike Hailwood
later in the season. The bike also has the
distinction of holding the all-time lap record
at Osmaston Manor.*

1954 BSA Gold Flash 650cc, fully restored.
£2,000–2,300 *BCB*

c1954/55 BSA Bantam D3 150cc, restored.
£500–600 *BCB*

1954 BSA Gold Star 250cc Road Racer,
rebuilt to original specification, excellent
condition throughout.
£4,200–4,500 *S*

*This machine was both road raced and scrambled by
Michael Martin. Back in the mid-1950's, Roland
Pike, an engineer and road racer of no mean ability,
joined BSA and ran a small 'race workshop' next door
to the experimental department at BSA's Small Heath
works. One of the projects which emerged from that
shop was a small run of about six specially
manufactured 250cc Gold Star Road Racers. This
machine, from the collection of the late Bill Howard,
is one of these rare bikes. As the 250cc Gold Stars
were never offered for sale to the general public, this
is a particularly rare example.*

1955 BSA B31 350cc, original
specification, rebuilt magneto, good
running order, old buff log book.
Est. £1,500–1,700 *S*

1955 BSA A10R Road Rocket, finished in
red with a black frame, restored, fitted with
new rims and exhaust system.
Est. £1,600–2,000 *S*

1956 BSA Gold Star Model ZB 32 350cc,
fully restored.
£3,300–3,500 *MR*

1956 BSA B31 Solo 350cc, finished in
dark green livery, museum stored.
Est. £1,400–1,800 *S*

*This bike has had only three owners
having been bought new by the
Southampton Fire Brigade, and being
first registered to The Secretary of State
at the Home Office.*

1956 BSA B33 500cc,
not standard.
£1,200–1,400 *BCB*

1956 BSA C11G 250cc, painted in maroon with
tank in polished aluminium and maroon.
£450–600 *S*

*This BSA 250 single is of the type introduced for the
1954 season and was kept in production for only
two years.*

1957 BSA C12 250cc, good cosmetic condition,
mechanical state unknown, complete and
apparently to original specification.
Est. £400–450 *S*

1957 BSA 650 A10 Gold Flash, with
plunger suspension.
£1,850–2,000 *AT*

1957 BSA Bantam 150cc.
£550–700 *VER*

1957 BSA Gold Star 350cc DB Engine,
BTH Magneto.
£3,000–4,000 *CBr*

1957 BSA C12 250cc, restored.
£700–900 *BCB*

1958 BSA A10 650cc, not totally original, engine overhauled, good working order.
£1,300–1,500 *CStC*

1959 BSA C15 250cc, overhead valve, unit-construction single, coil ignition/alternator.
£600–800 *RJES*

Made at Armoury Road in Birmingham, this model was inspired by Edward Turner's Triumph Tiger Cub, from which it was developed. Like the Cub it was low and light with good handling and easy starting. It was a considerable advance on the earlier 250 singles made by the company.

1959 BSA DBD 34 Gold Star 500cc.
£7,500–8,000 *VER*

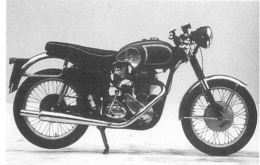

1960 BSA DBD 34 Gold Star 500cc, original 'Café Racer', clip-on handlebars, rear-set footrests, close ratio gears, 1⅜in Amal GP carburettor and racing cam profiles, optional 4½ gallon light alloy tank.
£7,000–8,000 *RJES*

The 'Clubmans' Gold Star gained its reputation when it dominated the Clubmans Racing Class in the Isle of Man in the Fifties.

1960 BSA A7 Shooting Star 500cc Twin, near original condition.
£1,700–2,000 *MR*

1961 BSA D1 Bantam 125cc.
£500–600 *VER*

1962 BSA DBD 34 Gold Star 500cc, excellent condition.
£7,000–8,000 *RCMC*

1963 BSA A50 500cc, in original condition.
£1,200–1,500 *BCB*

1964 BSA US Model A65 Rocket Clubman's 650cc Solo, OHV, air-cooled, 4 stroke, vertical twin, 75mm bore, 74mm stroke, 4 speed gearbox, chain final drive, telescopic front forks, pivoted fork rear suspension, factory café racer with dropped handlebars and humped seat.
£2,000–2,500 *OxM*

1965 BSA Lightning 650cc, restored.
£2,300–2,700 *BCB*

1967 BSA Spitfire.
£3,000–3,500 *AtMC*

1965 BSA 650cc Lightning Clubman.
£3,000–6,000 *WCM*

This model was made for only 10 months, and is now rare.

1967 BSA Spitfire MkIII 650cc.
£2,500–3,250 *WCM*

1967 BSA Bantam Supreme 175cc.
£300–400 *PS*

1972 BSA Rocket 3 750cc, finished in red and black, paintwork and mechanics in good condition, in original condition throughout with no known modifications from catalogue specification.
Est. £2,400–2,600 *S*

1971/1972 BSA B50SS Gold Star 500cc Unit Single.
£1,500–2,000 *RCMC*

This is not really a 'Goldie', but it was BSA's last effort before closing down in 1973, and is becoming rare.

CAPRIOLO (Italian)

1954 Capriolo Sport 75, single cylinder face cam engine with in-unit 4 speed gearbox, painted in red and black, pressed steel frame, telescopic forks and plunger rear suspension, totally restored, excellent condition all-round.
Est. £1,500–1,700 *S*

Built by Aer Caproni SpA of Trento, Italy and later Aeromere SpA, the once famous aircraft builders, Capriolo machines were made from 1948 until 1963.

COTTON (British)

A bike design with characteristic triangular straight tubes was patented by F. W. Cotton in the early 1900s. Shortly afterwards he began to make motorcycles with Villiers 2 strokes and ohv Blackburne engines.

Despite a successful racing history, the company ceased trading in 1939. After WWII the company was sold and newly designed Cottons were once again equipped with Villiers engines. However, when a shortage of Villiers engines occurred production eventually came to a halt once again in 1980.

1923 Cotton 342cc, good black, green and blue paintwork, mechanically very good, original machine, featuring Cotton's triangulated frame construction, with old log book.
Est. £2,200–3,000 *S*

COVENTRY (British)

CORGI (British)

The tiny scooters made by Brockhouse Engineering of Southport were unique in that they were folding scooters, designed to be dropped by parachute during WWII.

1950 Brockhouse Corgi 98cc, red paintwork, in original condition throughout with good mechanics, with old log book.
£350–450 *S*

1948 Brockhouse Corgi 98cc, finished in red and black, very good mechanical condition, no known deviations from catalogue specification, original log book.
£450–550 *S*

Developed from the wartime Welbike, the Corgi offered cheap transport, could be stored in a small space due to its small size and folding handlebars, and became popular as city transport.

1934 Coventry-Eagle K2 Sports 250cc, finished in black and red, good overall condition, features an Albion 3 speed gearbox, pressed steel frame, good running order.
£600–800 *S*

1932 Coventry-Eagle Midget 98cc Villiers 2 Stroke Single Cylinder, finished in black and cream, restored to high standard both mechanically and cosmetically, 2 speed hand change Albion gearbox.
£900–1,000 *S*

DOT *(British)*

Known for its production of many successful motocross and trials machines, DOT was founded in Manchester by racing motorcyclist Harry Reed.

DOT'S were generally fitted with Bradshaw and JAP engines from 246cc to 986cc V-twins, and then later fitted with Villiers 2 stroke engines. Despite an envious racing record, DOT ceased production in 1932, but commenced operations again in 1948, only to disband in 1974.

1964 DOT Trials, 37A square barrel engine, new alloy guards.
£850–900 *CBr*

1955 DOT, with Bultaco tank, Villiers 6E with 3 speed gearbox, very rare.
£650–700 *CBr*

1965 DOT 250cc, Alpha engine, totally restored.
£1,500–1,700 *CBr*

DOUGLAS *(British)*

c1920 Douglas, 2¾hp.
£4,000–4,500 *AtMC*

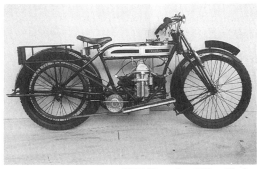

1921 Douglas 350cc Twin.
£4,000–4,500 *VER*

1957 Douglas Dragonfly 348cc, only 300 miles since rebuild, very good condition throughout with no known alterations from original catalogue specification.
£2,800–3,000 *S*

Douglas announced their new model, the Dragonfly, in 1955, forsaking their torsion bar rear suspension and radiodraulic front forks for a pivoted fork rear frame and Earles type front forks.

1951 Douglas MkV OHV Horizontally Opposed Twin 348cc, in very good but unrestored condition, lacking only tool box lid, a magneto bolt and exhaust support stays, original handbook and buff log book.
£1,250–1,400 *PS*

DUCATI *(Italian)*

Despite Ducati's glamorous image of today, the company's first motorcycle was actually an auxiliary 49cc 4 stroke engine unit, called the Cucciolo, designed to fit ordinary pedal cycles. Their micro engines paved the way for Ducati's range of small motorcycles which were produced in the early 50s. In May 1954 Fabio Taglioni joined the Ducati team as Chief Designer and promptly developed a series of overhead cam singles, followed by the Desmo models later in the 60s. Other classics included the 750 V-twin and 900SS. Ducati's road-going motorcycles have reflected the Italian company's pedigree, and as a result these high performance machines have always been sought after.

1971 Ducati Monza Junior 160cc, finished in red, 12 volt electrical system, completely rebuilt.
£850–1,000 *S*

1966 Ducati Sebring 350cc American Model, OHC single cylinder.
£800–1,000 *PC*

1972 Ducati 450cc Scrambler, good original condition, finished in yellow and black.
£2,200–2,500 *COYS*

1974 Ducati 250 MkIII, overhauled and resprayed in the Italian racing colours of red with green, excellent condition.
£1,500–1,800 *COYS*

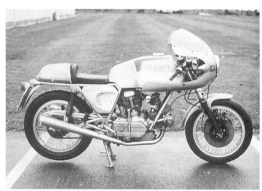

1975 Ducati 750cc Super Sport, desmodromic valve gear, paintwork and upholstery good, electrics as new, 5 speed gearbox and transmission reconditioned, excellent condition.
£6,400–6,800 *S*

1960 Aermacchi Ala Verde Sports 250cc Roadster.
£2,500–3,000 *AtMC*

1968 Aermacchi Ala D'oro 250cc.
£10,000–10,500 *AtMC*

1938 AJS V-Twin 1000cc.
£6,250–6,500 *VER*

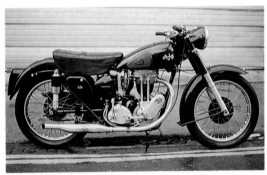

1954 AJS 18S 500cc, restored.
£1,800–2,000 *BCB*

c1957 AJS 350cc Trials Bike.
£2,800–3,000 *AtMC*

1934 Ariel De Luxe 500cc, twin port, totally restored.
£13,000–13,350 *EM*

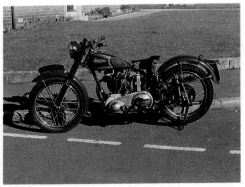

1953 Ariel 350cc.
£2,250–2,500 *PM*

1976 BMW R90S.
£3,800–4,000 *AtMC*

1929 BSA Sloper 500cc.
£2,400–2,900 *CBr*

1933 BSA Sports 350cc.
£3,000–3,400 *PM*

1933 BSA B1 250cc, side valve, restored.
£1,000–1,200 *BCB*

1934 BSA B2 250cc.
£2,000–2,750 *AtMC*

c1940 BSA M20 500cc, side valve single.
£1,500–1,800 *RCMC*
*Used during WWII for convoy duty and by the
'Desert Rats'. Slow but very reliable.*

1940 BSA M20.
£1,200–1,500 *MVT*
*This model was used for many years
by the British Army.*

1951 BSA B31 350cc.
£1,500–2,000 *RCMC*

1952 BSA D1 Bantam 125cc, original unrestored, in
running order.
£450–500 *BCB*

1956 BSA DBD 34 Gold Star.
£6,000–6,750 *AtMC*

1958 BSA A10 Spitfire Replica.
£2,000–2,500 *RCMC*

A good copy of the model made for export to the west coast of the USA. An original would be worth twice as much as this one.

1959 BSA A10 Super Rocket.
£2,250–2,500 *RCMC*

1960 BSA Gold Flash 650cc, rebuilt and now in good condition.
£2,000–2,500 *MR*

1961 BSA C15 250cc, original.
£600–800 *BCB*

1972 BSA Rocket 3.
£3,200–3,650 *VER*

1962 BSA A10 Golden Flash 650cc.
£2,000–2,500 *RCMC*

1972 BSA Rocket 3 750cc.
£3,250–3,500 *AtMC*

1929 Brough-Superior SS80.
£13,000–13,500   *AtMC*

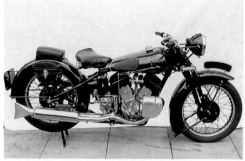

c1938 Brough-Superior Model 1150, restored.
£12,000–14,000   *CBr*

1930 Brough-Superior SS80 1000cc.
£13,500–14,000   *VER*

1932 Brough-Superior 680, Overhead Valve.
£15,500–16,000   *AtMC*

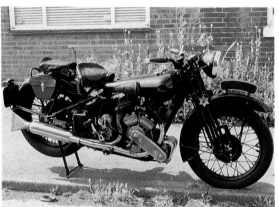

c1938 Brough-Superior SS80 1000cc.
£11,000–12,000   *AtMC*

1973 Bultaco Persang Mk 8 Motocross.
£650–750   *CBr*

1964 Cotton Trials Villiers 37A 250cc,
totally original.
£850–1,000   *CBr*

1973 CCM 500 Motocross, in poor condition.
£1,000–1,250   *CBr*

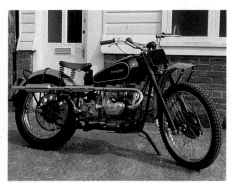

1950 Douglas T35 Competition Model.
£2,000–3,000 *RCMC*
These motorcycles were built to order by
Douglas using WWII frames.

1928 Douglas DT Speedway Bike.
£9,000–10,000 *AtMC*

1959 Ducati 200 Elite.
£1,700–1,900 *PM*

1974 Ducati 750 Sport.
£4,500–5,000 *AtMC*

1975 Ducati 125 Regolarita 2 Stroke Enduro.
£1,850–2,000 *PC*
This machine was ridden by Pat Slinn in
1975 ISDT.

1975 Ducati Desmo 350cc.
£2,000–2,500 *PM*

1978 Ducati 900SS.
£5,500–5,700 *EM*

1973 Dunstall Honda 900/4, unrestored
original condition.
£2,200–2,500 *BKS*
This is the 1973 Los Angeles Show model.

1936 Excelsior Manxman 250cc.
£7,500–8,000 *VER*

c1937 Excelsior Manxman 250cc.
£8,000–8,500 *AtMC*

1910 FN, 4 cylinders.
£10,000–10,500 *AtMC*

1957 Excelsior 98cc.
£300–350 *PM*

1930 Francis-Barnett Pulman, 2 cylinders.
£3,500–4,000 *AtMC*

1957 Francis-Barnett Villiers 8E, 4 speed,
totally restored.
£1,500–1,650 *CBr*

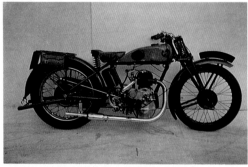

1924 Grindlay-Peerless 500cc.
£3,500–3,800 *VER*

1927 Grindlay-Peerless.
£19,000–20,000 *AtMC*
This machine is a rare Brooklands racer.

1965 Greeves Scrambler Challenger 250cc,
with Cerani forks.
£1,500–1,700   *CBr*

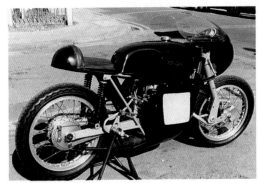

1968 Greeves Oulton 350cc.
£4,500–5,000   *AtMC*
One of only 21 built.

1970 Greeves Griffon 380cc.
£1,250–1,500   *CBr*
This bike is one of the last of only 250 built.

1929 Henderson, restored.
£9,500–10,000   *AtMC*

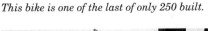

1973 Hercules 300cc, Wankel engine made
under NSU patents by Sachs, horizontal
engine coupled to in-unit gearbox with chain
final drive, restored.
£900–1,200   *RJES*

1938 HRD Series A Rapide.
£28,000–30,000   *AtMC*
One of only 70 built.

1948 HRD Series B Black Shadow.
£15,000–16,000   *AtMC*

1949 HRD Vincent Series C Rapide.
£11,500–12,000   *VER*

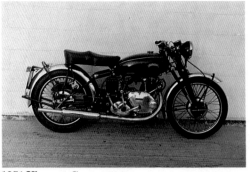

1951 Vincent Comet 500cc.
£4,250–5,000 *AT*

1951 Vincent Comet 500cc, restored.
£5,000–6,000 *BCB*

1952 Vincent Comet 500cc.
£4,500–5,000 *VER*

c1952 Vincent Comet 500cc.
£4,500–5,000 *AtMC*

1953 Vincent Rapide Tourer, built to USA
specification.
£12,000–12,500 *AtMC*

c1954 Vincent Series C Black Shadow.
£14,500–15,000 *AtMC*

1955 Vincent Series D Rapide.
£11,500–12,000 *AtMC*

1955 Vincent Prince 1000cc V-Twin.
£15,000–15,500 *VER*

1957 Norton Manx 350cc.
£9,000–10,000 *VER*

1960 Norton 350cc Model 50.
£3,000–3,500 *PM*

1961 Norton 99SS Café Racer,
totally restored.
£2,500–3,000 *CRMC*

1958 Norton 600cc Café Racer, not standard.
£1,800–2,000 *BCB*

1965 Norton 650SS.
£2,300–2,600 *BCB*

1971 Norton Commando 750cc, restored.
£5,500–5,800 *EM*

1975 Norton Commando 850cc, with
Norvil body.
£5,000–5,250 *EM*

1975 Norton Commando Mk III 850cc.
£2,600–2,900 *AT*

1934 Panther Redwing 600cc.
£3,500–4,000 *AtMC*

1955 Panther 250cc.
£1,400–1,600 *PM*

1924 Raleigh V-Twin 800cc.
£9,000–10,000 *AtMC*

1948 Peugeot 125cc 2 Stroke.
£425–550 *AT*

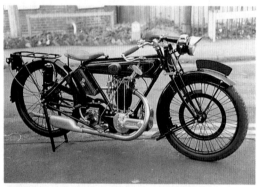

1926 Raleigh Sport 350cc, overhead valve.
£4,250–4,500 *AtMC*

1928 Raleigh Model 23 498cc, excellent condition.
£3,000–4,000 *S*

1928 Raleigh 250cc.
£1,800–2,000 *VER*

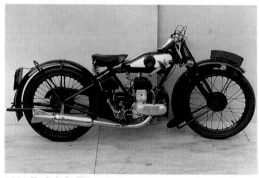

1930 Raleigh SV 298cc.
£1,800–2,000 *VER*

1903 Rex.
£8,000–9,000 *VER*

1972 Rickman 175cc Zündapp Engine,
good condition.
£650–800 *CBr*

1950 Rotax-JAP Speedway Bike, overhead valve.
£3,000–3,500 *AtMC*

1974 Rickman Honda KZ 750cc.
£2,000–3,000 *WCM*

1916 Royal Enfield 675cc, 3 cylinders.
£20,000+ *AtMC*

1940 Royal Enfield WD/C 350cc, side valve.
£1,200–1,500 *MVT*

This model was later replaced by the overhead valve WD/CO.

1941 Royal Enfield WD/CO 350cc, restored.
£1,500–1,750 *BCB*

1944 Royal Enfield WD/RE 125cc, 2 stroke.
£800–1,200 *MVT*

Considered to be unreliable, needing frequent rubber band changes on forks. Civilian post-war models are worthless and often altered to WD specification, so be careful when buying.

1955 Royal Enfield Bullet 350cc Trials Bike.
£1,000–1,200 *MR*

1957 Royal Enfield Bullet 350cc.
£2,500–3,000 *AtMC*

c1959 Royal Enfield Crusader 250cc.
£2,000–2,500 *AtMC*

1957 Royal Enfield 150 Prince.
£400–600 *PM*

1961 Royal Enfield Clipper 350cc, restored.
£1,250–1,350 *CBr*

1965 Royal Enfield Interceptor 750cc,
totally restored.
£7,500–8,000 *EM*

1965 Royal Enfield GT Continental 250cc,
restored.
£1,200–1,500 *BCB*

c1970 Royal Enfield 250cc Sports,
fibreglass fuel tank, 4 speed gears, engine not
original, very good condition throughout.
£1,300–1,400 *S*

EXCELSIOR (British)

1936 Excelsior Manxman Model F11 248cc,
excellent condition.
£5,300–5,600 *S*

1935 Excelsior Manxman Model ER12 350cc,
overhead camshaft, touring carburettor and
magneto, racing fuel tank and alloy brake plates,
Albion 4 speed gearbox, finished in black and red,
excellent condition throughout.
£5,500–5,800 *S*

1946 Excelsior 98cc Autobyk, Villiers
Junior De Luxe engine with one gear, rigid
suspension front and rear, museum stored.
£100–150 *S*

*Excelsiors made very basic and economical
post-war machines, which included the
Autobyk and the Universal.*

1945 Replica Excelsior Welbike Mk II,
£1,000–1,200 *MVT*

*As so few originals survived, replicas now probably
outnumber them. This model has a front brake,
unlike the originals.*

FRANCIS-BARNETT (British)

The Coventry based factory was established in
1919. The first bikes produced had 293cc and
346cc sv JAP engines. Later Villiers and JAP
engines were used on the triangular framed
motorcycles. In the 1950s AMC bought out the
Coventry factory, and eventually moved to
Birmingham where, in 1964, both AMC and
Francis-Barnett production was ceased.

1951 Francis-Barnett 197cc Trials,
Villiers 2 stroke engine, rebuilt, very
good condition.
Est. £850–950 *S*

*The 1950s trials scene is best
remembered for people like Sammy
Miller on his big Ariel and Gordon
Jackson on the AJS 4 stroke singles,
small 2 strokes which, with their low
weight and low cost, predominated in the
smaller capacity classes. One of the most
successful manufacturers during this
period was Francis-Barnett, whose works
team met with considerable success, with
the result that many of the innovations
that they made found their way on to
production bikes.*

c1951 Frances-Barnett 197cc, believed
to be a Falcon model 81 fitted with the
Villiers 10E single cylinder two stroke
engine, good condition throughout.
Est. £300–400 *S*

*Along with their partners in the AMC
group, James and Francis-Barnett are
best remembered for their post-war
lightweights that provided cheap,
basic transport.*

1954 Francis-Barnett Falcon 58 Single Cylinder 2 Stroke 197cc, Villiers 8E engine with 3 speed gearbox, original condition.
£500–600 *PS*

This is a good example of a once very popular lightweight 2 stroke.

1955 Francis-Barnett 150cc, single cylinder 2 stroke engine in a loop frame, telescopic forks and plunger rear suspension, good condition finished in black with gold pinstriping.
£300–450 *S*

This machine is typical of Francis-Barnett's post-war utility production.

1963 Francis-Barnett Model 96 150cc, AMC designed engine, 3 speed gearbox.
£500–700 *RJES*

Locate the Source
The source of each illustration in Miller's can be found by checking the code letters below each caption with the list of contributors.

1965 Francis-Barnett Falcon, restored, good condition.
£650–800 *MR*

GILERA *(Italian)*

1949 Gilera San Remo Racer.
£8,000–10,000 *PC*

c1954 Gilera Saturno 500cc, finished in red and white, straight through exhaust pipe and dropped handlebars, excellent running order, non-standard.
£750–900 *S*

Comparable to BSA's Gold Star model, the Gilera Saturno, introduced before WWII, had a long and successful career in all areas of motorcycling competition. Featuring a 500cc overhead valve single cylinder engine and a fully sprung frame, it offered the durability and performance required by even the most demanding clubman.

1964 Gilera 125 6-Day Special, good condition.
£800–1,000   PC

GODDEN (British)

Godden 500cc Grass Track, Weslake engine,
good cosmetic order with a nickel plated frame
and blue paintwork, Benly gearbox, brakes
and rear suspension.
Est. £970–1,000   S

*Literally one of the 'grass root' forms of motorcycle
sport, grass track has been responsible for producing
many great riders, who have dominated national
and international speedway and longtrack events, as
well as providing exciting and close racing for
spectators in rural areas. The machines traditionally
utilise British single cylinder 4 stroke engines such
as Weslake's, although engines provided by the
Italians and, most notably, Czech Jawa engines have
also been used.*

GREEVES (British)

1964 Greeves 197cc Trials, Villiers 2 stroke
engine and 4 speed gearbox, finished in blue with
polished alloy cycle parts, mechanically good
condition, Greeves unusual cast alloy front frame
member and leading link front forks.
Est. £600–700   S

1977 Gilera TG1 125cc, 2 stroke engine,
5 speed gearbox.
£500–600   PC

GRINDLAY-PEERLESS (British)

Grindlay Ltd., established in 1923, originally
manufactured sidecars before producing their
first motorcycles, which carried 190cc JAP
single cylinder and 996cc Barr & Stroud
sleeve-valve V-twin engines. Grindlay-Peerless
also used the Rudge Python engine, a
convenient move considering the Rudge
factory was only yards away. Despite the short
production span of Grindlay-Peerless
motorcycles (1923–34), they won many road
races and hill climb awards.

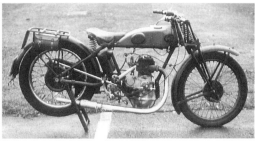

1924 Grindlay-Peerless 499cc, in running order.
£2,900–3,200   S

HAGON

c1961 Hagon JAP 4 Stud 500cc Grass Track Racer, 1948 overhead valve engine, 2 speed Norton gearbox, nickelled frame, mudguards, excellent condition throughout.
Est. £1,200–1,300 *S*

1943 Harley-Davidson WLC 750cc, V-twin, side valve engine, Canadian army specification.
£4,000–5,000 *MVT*

This was the Canadian version of the WLA, which was also used by the RAF.

c1942 Harley-Davidson WLA 45 700cc, comprehensively rebuilt utilising both new and used parts, very good condition throughout, presented in military trim.
Est. £4,500–5,000 *S*

HARLEY-DAVIDSON
(American)

c1945 Harley-Davidson WLA 750cc Solo, side valve air-cooled 4 stroke engine, V-twin, 4 speed gearbox, chain final drive, springer front forks, rigid sub frame, hand gear change, foot clutch.
£2,000–2,500 *OxM*

1942 Harley-Davidson, finished in red, completely rebuilt and restored.
£5,700–6,000 *LF*

1947 Harley-Davidson FL1200, fully restored.
£9,000–11,000 *RCMC*

This was the first year of the pan head engine, which was used in various models right through to 1965, when it became the Electraglide.

c1953 Harley-Davidson Model 45.
Est. £5,000–5,500 *S*

1959 Harley-Davidson Duo-Glide 1200cc, V-twin pan head engine, 4 speed gearbox, good condition, paintwork in blue and white.
Est. £7,500–8,000 *S*

c1960 Harley-Davidson Sportster Custom, good condition.
£3,500–4,500 *RCMC*

- Built in both the US and Canada, the Harley-Davidson 45cu in, 3 speed, saw extensive use during WWII in virtually all of the Allied armies.
- In 1960 Harley-Davidson took over Aermacchi and vowed to continue their long-standing racing traditions, sweeping aside the previously strong Japanese challenge in the process.
- Harley-Davidson is one of the world's longest surviving marques, founded in 1903, and is still in production today.

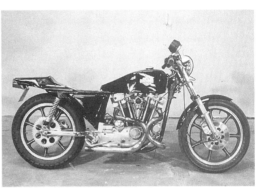

c1975/1976 Harley-Davidson 1000cc Prototype (Factory) Café Racer, V-twin engine, 4 speed gearbox, has many characteristics not found on production models, missing its fairing, indicators, seat cover, silencers, air filter and chain, it is nevertheless substantially complete, with parts and sales catalogue, service manual, some history and a letter from the factory.
Est. £3,750–4,000 *S*

First registered in the UK in January 1987, this is the third and last prototype built by the works before production commenced. Prior to this it was used in the USA for press and road tests, and to illustrate the service manuals and the main 1977 catalogue.

c1976 Harley-Davidson Aermacchi 250cc 2 Stroke Twin Racer, unrestored and in good original condition, good running order, with racing spares including barrels and matching pistons, gaskets, and sprockets.
£6,000–8,000 *BKS*

> **Miller's is a price GUIDE not a price LIST**

1979 Harley-Davidson XLCR 1000, unrestored original Café Racer, rare.
£4,000–5,000 *RCMC*

1978 Harley-Davidson XR 750 Racer, all alloy engine, mainly used for long track racing in the U.S.A.
£5,000–7,000 *RCMC*

HONDA *(Japanese)*

Soichiro Honda converted surplus army 2 stroke engines into power bicycles after WWII. The easy sale of these bikes encouraged him to move into motorcycle design. Shortly after the incorporation of Honda Motor Co Ltd., in 1948, they produced over 3,500 98cc Model D 2 strokes and by 1953 produced 32,000 Model E 4 strokes.

Despite increasing production numbers, Honda realised that to survive it would have to export its machines on a grand scale. To achieve this, Honda used a combined strategy based on clever advertising, producing world championship winners, and manufacturing smaller, efficient, but reliable bikes at affordable prices. This recipe for success appeared to work, and by the mid-1960s Honda's production levels for all its models was no less than 130,000 bikes per month.

c1962 Honda CR110 50cc DOHC.
£18,000–20,000 *AtMC*

1964 Honda C77 305cc, painted in dark blue, with red upholstery, excellent original condition throughout, pressed steel forks, with Duplex springing, and swinging arm rear suspension.
£2,000–2,300 *S*

1964 Honda CB 77 305cc, correct black and chrome livery with black upholstery, excellent concours condition throughout, no alternations to maker's original specification.
£2,000–2,500 *S*

1965 Honda ST50 Monkey Bike, original paint finish with all original features, rigid frame, low seat, detachable handlebars, running order, complete, original log book.
£1,200–1,400 *BKS*

c1965 Honda CR93.
£15,000+ *AtMC*

1967 Honda C177 305cc, American import street scrambler, twin cylinders, twin leading shoe brakes, completely original.
£1,500–2,500 *GLC*

1968 Honda CB450 K1, finished in the correct black and silver paintwork, good condition cosmetically with good mechanics.
£1,200–1,400 *S*

- Honda's angular 125cc twin was introduced in 1959 and offered performance that was comparable to many sporting 250s.
- Very few C77 305cc twins with overhead cams were imported from Japan into the UK.
- Production of the CB450 Black Bomber in 1965 was Honda's answer to large capacity machines.
- The Honda Gold Wing, introduced in 1975, had water-cooled transverse-mounted flat 4 engines and was their top of the range model.

1970 Honda CB750, excellent condition with no known modifications from catalogue specification.
Est. £3,000–4,500 *S*

1970 Honda CB750, finished in Candy Ruby Red, excellent condition throughout, restored.
Est. £3,500–4,000 *S*

1973 Honda 70cc, red and black paintwork in fair condition, mechanical condition unknown.
£300–500 *S*

1973 Honda SL125 Trail, single cylinder 122cc 4 stroke engine with overhead camshaft, 5 speed, good condition.
Est. £2,400–2,600 *S*

1976 Honda CB 400/4, overhead cam 4 cylinder engine, good running order, dropped handlebars, converted to monoshock rear end.
£250–350 *S*

1976 Honda Gold Wing 1000cc, good condition throughout, fully equipped including panniers.
Est. £2,200–2,600 *S*

1977 Honda CR125 M3 Elsinore Scrambler, 6 speed constant mesh gearbox, good condition
Est. £2,000–2,200 *S*

1979 Honda TL 250cc Trials, magnesium cases, very rare.
£1,000–1,400 *CBr*

HRD (British)

Founded in 1924 in Wolverhampton by TT winner Howard Raymond Davies, HRD Motors produced high quality sporting motorcycles using frames produced in-house and specially built JAP engines.

The model 90 features a single port 500cc JAP engine and the Super 90 a twin port racing JAP engine with a top speed approaching 100mph. All models feature hand change 3 speed Burman gearboxes. Approximately 1,000 HRDs were built in Wolverhampton but less than 20 machines are thought to still exist.

HRD Motors went into receivership in 1927, but the machines continued to be built until early 1928. The name and assets were bought from the receiver by Ernie Humphries who then sold them on to Cambridge undergraduate P. C. Vincent. He had long been an admirer of HRD machines and needed an established name for the machines he was about to produce. These new machines were Vincent-HRDs featuring Vincent's patented rear suspension and using JAP and Rudge engines.

Vincent-HRDs continued to use proprietary engines until a disastrous showing at the 1934 TT when the special JAP engines proved unreliable. Phil Irving and Phil Vincent, then designed the 500cc engine for the Series A machines.

1938 HRD Series A.
£8,250–9,000 *ATC*

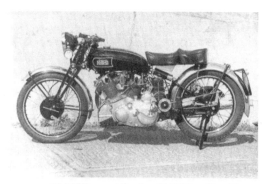

1947 Vincent Series B 1000cc Rapide,
Miller lighting, Lucas cut-out and charging kit, fully restored, low mileage, very good condition throughout.
Est. £9,000–11,000 *S*

This example of Vincent's classic Rapide was exported to France when new, returning to the U.K. in the mid-1950s.

c1950 Vincent HRD Lightning 1000cc.
£40,000+ *AtMC*
One of only 29 built.

1949 Vincent HRD Rapide.
£7,500–12,000 *WCM*

1951 Vincent Series C 1000 Black Shadow.
£13,000–17,000 *WCM*

1952 Vincent Shadow Series C, good condition cosmetically, chromium plated steel wheel rims.
Est. £8,500–9,750 *S*

1952 Vincent Series C 1000cc, engine rebuilt recently, alloy rims and 12 volt electrics, excellent condition throughout.
£9,500–10,500 *S*

1952 Vincent Montlhéry Record Breaker.
£23,000–25,000 *AtMC*

1953 Vincent Comet 500cc, engine extensively rebuilt including new cylinder heads and barrels, good paintwork, fully functioning Lucas electrical system, no known modifications from standard.
£5,200–5,500 *S*

1955 Vincent Series D Rapide 1000cc, V-twin engine, fully restored.
£10,000–12,000 *BCB*

1955 Vincent Black Prince 1000cc, rebuilt, frame restored and fibreglass panelling repainted in black.
£11,600–12,000 *S*

1954/1969 Egli Vincent 998cc Solo Racer, new primary drive belt, Mk II cams, reworked input ducts, 40mm smooth bore Amals and carefully determined exhaust pipe lengths which have a critical bearing on the engine's performance with the aid of the Ledar dyno, set of 38mm Marzocchi forms and Lockheed brakes, original log book.
Est. £20,000–25,000 *S*

Few racing machines' histories are as well known as this particular example, partly because few machines have remained in their creators' hands for 24 years. Indeed, it is reputedly the first Vincent to compete in a major event at Daytona raceway taking 19th place in the 1988 Battle of Twins event.

HUMBER (British)

1922 Humber 4½hp Flat Twin Solo, correctly finished in black enamel, with gold lines, nickel plated fittings, acetylene headlamp, tyre pump and leather panniers.
£9,200–9,500 *S*

Humber's post war offering in 1920 maintained their flat twin tradition, but the new machine of 4½hp reverted to air cooling. This machine was restored some eighteen years ago, having been discovered in original condition in a garage where it had been untouched since 1931. Since restoration it has taken part in two Banbury Runs winning First Class awards and in 1986 won the concours award in the Banbury Run for the best early vintage bike.

INDIAN (American 1901, British 1951–63)

Indian produced its first model, the single in 1904 and established the company's reputation for sophisticated design and excellent quality which was to stand for many decades. With an eye to exports Indian entered four riders in the Senior TT on the Mountain circuit in 1911. Placing 1-2-3, with the help of its new 2 speed gearboxes, Indian's name was made in Europe and in the following year over 20,000 machines were exported. By 1919 the Scout, a 600cc side-valve, was introduced and was soon followed by the Chief – an uprated Powerplus – and the 1200cc Big Chief.

The introduction of tariffs in the UK and cheap motor cars in the mid-20s eroded Indian's profits. However, they did manage to acquire the Ace company but were taken over themselves in 1930 by E. P. Du Pont. With profits still plunging, money was injected into the company by British entrepreneur John Brockhouse. Brockhouse assumed control of Indian in 1949 but it was not until 1953 that production in the USA was terminated. New machines followed but were unsuccessful with many of the final models being merely re-badged imports.

1948 Indian Chief, finished in correct Indian Red, complete engine rebuild and restoration to original specification, original certificate of title from the State of Kansas, very good condition.
£7,500–8,500 *COYS*

HUSQVARNA (Swedish)

1973 Husqvarna 125cc Motocross, complete, unrestored condition.
£250–300 *CBr*

1911 Indian V-Twin 7/9hp Racer.
£30,000+ *FHF*

1942 Indian 741B 500cc V-Twin.
£3,000–4,000 *MVT*
This was one of the most common motorcycles of WWII.

1958 Indian Chief 700cc, Royal Enfield twin cylinder engine, and other components, painted blue and beige, excellent condition.
Est. £8,000–8,500 *S*

Some 55 were built, of which some 50 went to the New York Police Department, and five were sold for civilian use. This is one of the very rare civilian versions.

ITOM *(Italian)*

c1960/1962 50cc Road Racer, new bearings and
oil seals, red and white paintwork, good overall
condition, racing tank and seat made as a 'one-off',
new and original Dunlop racing tyres, rev-counter
up to 12,000 rpm with drive, and wider front brake
shoes fitted.
£900–1,000 *S*

IZ *(Russian)*

1954 IZ 350cc, finished in blue, original condition,
imported from Poland and likely to have seen some
military service.
Est. £400–600 *S*

*This is believed to be an example of a Russian built
IZ 350cc 2 stroke twin, the design for which was
copied from DKW's excellent military 350cc.*

JAMES *(British)*

The first James produced in 1902 consisted
of a Minerva engine in a standard cycle frame.
The company was moved to Birmingham in
1908 and produced a series of lightweight
machines which were popular with the
military in WWII. They also produced
successful trials bikes, most of which were
powered by either 197 or 246cc 2 stroke
engines. AMC purchased James in 1951 and
attempted unsuccessfully to produce a James
scooter. Production of the James marque
ceased in 1964.

1929 James 172cc, finished in black with metallic
brown fuel tank, with rear carrier, good condition.
Est. £1,300–1,500 *S*

*The late 1920s saw many established 4 stroke
manufacturers adding lightweight 2 strokes to
their range to account for the increasingly hostile
economic climate.*

1950 James Comet 98cc.
£350–400 *MR*

> **Miller's is a price GUIDE
> not a price LIST**

1953 James Trials, rigid frame
Villiers 197 engine 4 speed
gearbox, rebuilt, not quite original.
£1,000–1,500 *CBr*

1957 James 197cc, AMC
engine, no silencer.
£750–850 *CBr*

1963 James Cadet 150cc AMC engine, finished in red, with a chrome exhaust system and fittings, good original condition.
£200–300 *S*

JAWA *(Czechoslovakian)*

c1970 Jawa 500cc, 2 valve 4 stroke engine, with oil bearing frame.
Est. £1,600–1,800 *S*
Used in competitions up to 1993.

KAWASAKI *(Japanese)*

Considered late starters among motorcycle manufacturers, Kawasaki's first serious move into the market was to take over production of the Meguro, a BSA A7 500cc lookalike in 1961. In 1962 Kawasaki introduced its first all Kawasaki B8 125cc 2 stroke range which sold well in the USA as did the gas guzzling H1 series which became somewhat of a cult motorcycle. With the passing of anti-pollution legislation, Kawasaki designed the Z1 range in 1972 with its transverse in line air-cooled 4 cylinder engine which was popular in the US.

c1974 Kawasaki H1 Mach III 500cc, finished in two tone green with the usual bright parts, in excellent original condition, with a Swansea V5.
£1,300–1,500 *S*

1975 Kawasaki Z 900 903cc Transverse 4 Cylinder 4 stroke, finished in maroon, good condition throughout.
£4,100–4,500 *S*

Make the most of Miller's

Condition is absolutely vital when assessing the value of a Classic Motorcycle. Top class bikes on the whole appreciate much more than less perfect examples. However, a rare, desirable machine may command a high price even when in need of restoration.

c1976 Kawasaki H1R 498.7cc, cantilever suspension, finished in distinctive lime green racing livery, with alloy rims.
£500–800 *S*

LAVERDA *(Italian)*

1972 Laverda 750 SF, robust sports twin, with large Laverda drum brakes.
£3,200–3,700 *PC*

1974 Laverda 750cc SFC Limited Production Street Racer, finished in orange, excellent condition.
£8,000–10,000 *PC*

> ## Locate the Source
> *The source of each illustration in Miller's can be found by checking the code letters below each caption with the list of contributors.*

1977 Laverda Jota 1000cc, 3 cylinders.
£15,000+ *PC*
This is the actual machine raced in the Avon Production Racing Series by Pete Davies, and is almost priceless.

1974 Laverda 250cc Chott, off-road enduro, rare.
£1,800–2,300 *PC*

MARTINSYDE *(British)*

LEVIS *(British)*

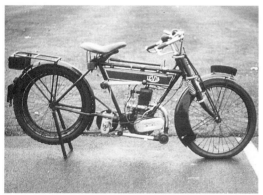

1914 Levis 211cc, countershaft gearbox and belt drive, black, with green tank, original specification throughout.
£1,800–2,100 *S*

1923 Martinsyde 347cc, fully restored, correct black and blue livery, excellent condition, no valancing on the front mudguard, some stainless fittings and an incorrect tyre pump, fully restored.
£8,100–8,500 *S*
This machine is believed to be the only extant single cylinder Martinsyde out of five machines produced.

MATCHLESS *(British)*

In 1901 Matchless initially made their motorcycles using De Dion and MMC engines. A decade later they switched to using JAP and MAG engines almost exclusively. Never known for their exciting designs, they were generally large and painted dull shades of khaki green. Despite this, the company was profitable and in 1931 acquired AJS. For a number of years, when parts for the two marques were rationalised, the bikes were virtually the same. Matchless went on to acquire Norton, Francis-Barnett and James and for the first time in many years persued the racing circuit.

This latest acquisition proved to be their downfall. The decision to manufacture a 2 stroke engine for James and Francis-Barnett proved disastrous, as did the decision to mix Norton and AMC parts to create special bikes for the US market. Shareholders revolted, designers resigned and by 1969 Matchless, effectively bankrupt, was sold to Manganese Bronze Holdings and Matchless simply disappeared until 1987.

1930 Matchless V3S 498cc, single cylinder overhead valve 4 stroke engine, black enamelled to original specification, comprehensive restoration with new chains and tyres, replacement bearings in the gearbox.
£4,000–4,300 *S*

1937 Matchless 500cc, Model G8 Sports, overhead valve, single cylinder, twin exhaust ports and horizontal carburettor, high-level exhaust system, chromium plated and painted tank containing the instruments and switches, centre stand, standard Burman gearbox and clutch.
£2,800–3,400 *RJES*

1938 Matchless 990cc Side Valve V-Twin Cylinder 4 stroke, finished in maroon with a chromium plated tank, fully rebuilt.
£5,000–5,400 *S*

1939 Matchless Model X 1000cc V-Twin, foot change and good brakes.
£6,000–8,000 *RCMC*

1941 Matchless G3L 350cc OHV, the first
British production motorcycle to be fitted with
'Teledraulic' forks.
£1,500–2,000 *MVT*

1946 Matchless G3L 350cc Single Cylinder,
fully restored.
£2,600–3,000 *DDM*

1946 Matchless G80 500cc.
£2,400–3,000 *WCM*

1949 Matchless G80 500cc OHV Single,
good original condition.
£2,200–2,600 *RCMC*

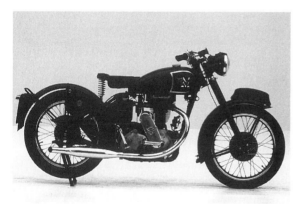

1949 Matchless G3L 350cc, 4 speed
Burman gearbox.
Est. £1,500–2,500 *RJES*

*This bike was the civilian version of
military model used during WWII.*

c1950 Matchless G80C 500cc Trials,
good condition.
Est. £1,500–2,000 *RCMC*

1952 Matchless 350cc Trials,
in running order.
£1,500–1,800 *MR*

1954 Matchless G9 500cc Super Clubman Twin,
unrestored, original condition, in running order.
£2,000–3,000 *RCMC*

1957 Matchless G3 LS 350cc, overhead valve single cylinder engine to standard bore, good black paintwork, good condition, telescopic front forks and sprung frame.
£1,400–1,600 *S*

1957 Matchless G3 LS 350cc, finished in black, sprung rear suspension, good all-round condition, all cycle parts ex-factory, old style brown log book and instruction manual, in regular use.
Est. £1,500–2,000 *LF*

The Radnorshire registration mark FO has the distinction of being the second slowest mark to be issued in the UK. The series started with FO1 in 1903 and reached FO9999 in 1958. It was beaten only by Rutland, whose FP series ran from 1903–60.

1958 Matchless G3 LS 350cc, in original condition.
£1,200–1,500 *BCB*

1958 Matchless G3 LCS
£3,750–4,000 *AtMC*

1960 Matchless Model G2 OHV Single Cylinder Scrambler 249cc, in good unrestored condition, fitted with all works modifications of that era.
£1,000–1,300 *PS*

1959 Matchless 650cc, in running order.
£1,300–1,500 *S*

Did you know?
MILLER'S Collectors Classic Motorcycles Price Guide *builds up year-by-year to form the most comprehensive photo library system available.*

1960 Matchless G5 348cc, red and black, good condition mechanically, restored, re-wired electrical system.
£1,100–1,500 *S*

1965 Matchless G85 500cc Scrambler.
£6,000–8,000 *CBr*

MOTO GUZZI *(Italian)*

In 1921, engineer Carlo Guzzi and enthusiast
Giorgio Parodi created the first horizontally
engined 500cc Moto Guzzi at Mandello del
Lario. By 1923, they were already famous in
racing, a title which continued to 1957 when
they withdrew from the sport for a time.
Thereafter, Moto Guzzi fell into financial
hardship, and briefly went into receivership.
The introduction of the 700cc V7 helped
alleviate Moto Guzzi's financial worries
temporarily. In 1971, it was sold to Allesandro
de Tomaso who has continued developing
Moto Guzzi.

MONET-GOYON *(French)*

The first Monet-Goyon produced in 1917
was in fact a wheel with a small engine that
could be attached to any bicycle. It was not
until 1930 that Monet-Goyon manufactured
its first motorcycle engine, a 344cc sv single.
After WWII it was followed by a 98cc, 124cc
and 232cc.

1929 Monet-Goyon Type BF 350cc, inlet
over exhaust, single cylinder, 4 stroke, black
and maroon, good condition throughout,
comprehensively restored.
£1,700–2,000 *S*

- **The Egretta featured a
  friction damped plunger
  type rear suspension 3 speed
  gearbox and a chromium
  plated petrol tank.**
- **In 1955 Moto Guzzi designed
  a most extraordinary and
  unsuccessful racing machine,
  the 500cc V-Eight.**
- **When post-war racing
  took off in 1949, Moto Guzzi
  set up an integrated factory
  racing department.**
- **Moto Guzzi were the first
  motorcycle marque to make
  use of wind tunnel facilities.**

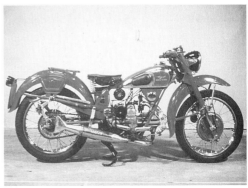

1937 Moto Guzzi PL 250 Egretta OHV Single,
finished in red with black lining, original in all
respects, good running order, with original Italian
registration plate.
Est. £1,700–2,000 *BKS*

1948 Moto Guzzi 498cc Military Super Alce.
£4,500–4,750 *AtMC*

1950 Moto Guzzi Airone 247cc, good
condition, fitted with new electrics,
wheels and tyres, new speedometer and
saddle, with sports carburettor
and speedometer.
£2,300–2,500 *S*

1955 Moto Guzzi Airone 247cc Turismo, good condition throughout. Est. **£3,000–4,000** *S*

1973 Moto Guzzi California, completely rebuilt, very rare. **£3,500–4,000** *CRMC*

MOTO MORINI

c1965 Moto Morini 124cc, good original condition, sporting styling with low handlebars and humped seat. **£600–700** *S*

Moto Morini met with considerable success in road racing with machines in the smaller classes, the benefits of which were applied to their road models.

1946/52 Moto Guzzi Super Alce 498cc, horizontal single cylinder engine, 4 speed gearbox, red paintwork in good condition, pillion seat, luggage carrier, auxilliary handlebars, full lighting set. **£4,200–4,800** *S*

MV AGUSTA *(Italian)*

Despite being manufacturers of helicopters, Meccanica Verghera (MV) have won more road racing world titles in every class between 125cc to 500cc than almost all other makes put together. The first MV, a 98cc 2 stroke, was produced in 1945 to fill a gap in the post-war shortage of transport. Within five years their first racing 4 stroke was created, a 124cc, ohc single with 4 speed with 3 gears and telescopic forks.

In stark contrast to their successful racing history, MV civilian bikes were non-inspirational. Initially focusing more on scooters than motorbikes, attempts to export their products, even the 4 cylinder road bikes, became a fruitless effort. In the late 70s the helicopter business had grown in importance and as a result the racing and road-going bikes ceased production.

1951 MV Agusta 124cc 2 stroke, fully restored, excellent condition throughout. **Est. £2,200–2,400** *S*

1956 MV Agusta Lusso 124cc, finished in red and black with red sides to the saddle, complete unrestored condition, leading link front fork with swinging arm rear suspension and an unsprung front mudguard, running order.
£300–400 *S*

1954 MV Agusta 172cc Disco Volante (Flying Saucer), finished in red and silver, full professional restoration, excellent condition.
£3,300–3,500 *S*

Featuring a duplex frame and Earles forks front suspension, the Disco Volante was a variant of MV's 175 touring and sports machines, and this machine dates from the first year in which 175s were introduced.

c1961 MV Agusta GT150, 4 stroke single cylinder engine with unit gearbox, housed in full loop frame with pivoted fork rear suspension and telescopic front forks, finished in red with a white flash and black frame, running order, new unused condition.
£1,200–1,500 *S*

MV Agusta manufactured an extensive range of sports and touring models of which this example is characteristic.

1968 MV Agusta 592cc 4 cylinder.
£9,000–10,000 *AtMC*

1972 MV Agusta B 349cc Electronica, original unrestored condition.
£700–1,000 *S*

1972 MV Agusta 125 Sports, single cylinder engine with in-unit 5 speed gearbox and racing saddle, good original condition.
£1,000–1,200 *S*

1976 MV Agusta 125 Sport.
£2,000–2,500 *AtMC*

MZ *(German)*

Motorad Zschopau was the successor to the IFA which was taken over in 1953 and superceded by the name MZ.

MZ produced a 125cc single and 250cc twin racer with disc valve induction. Two similar road machines were produced for both domestic sale and export at competitive prices. With the reunification of Germany, state support has been withdrawn and the company is experiencing difficulties.

1970 MZ 250cc Enduro, original works model.
£3,500–4,000 *PC*

c1973 MV Agusta 350S, in good running order with no known modifications.
£2,100–2,500 *S*

1976 MV Agusta 750S America.
£13,500–15,500 *WCM*

1978 MV Agusta 832 Monza.
£17,000–19,000 *WCM*

NEW GERRARD *(British)*

'Jock' Porter died at a relatively early age, but achieved a great deal in his short life. After serving in WWI he set up Porter's Motor Mart in Edinburgh, selling various makes of motorcycles. Then in 1922, he formed New Gerrard Motors in Edinburgh, and manufactured his own New Gerrard Motorcycles using Blackburne, Barr & Stroud sleeve valve engines, and later JAP engines.

1923/1924 New Gerrard 175cc Racer, unrestored, with a photograph of the trophy won in the 1924 Ultra Lightweight TT.
Est. £8,000–10,000 *S*

NEW HUDSON *(British)*

1925 New Hudson TT 500cc Supersports, single cylinder side valve engine, 3 speed gearbox, 'flat-tanker', finished in black, brown and gold, in excellent condition throughout with no known modifications from the standard specification.
£3,500–4,000 *S*

This is believed to be one of only two 1925 New Hudson's still surviving.

NORTON *(British)*

The Norton Manufacturing Company of Birmingham turned its attention to motorcycles in 1902, and the success of its machines over the years has been legendary. The first bikes were built using engines from other makes and it was not until 1907 that Norton designed its own engine. The 'long stroke' engines of 79 x 100mm, 490cc dimensions became a Norton tradition.

The success of Norton's sporting history with its many star riders did much to sell its road machines. However, in 1952 Norton was sold in anticipation of death duties by the Vandervell family to AMC. In 1962 the company was moved from Birmingham to the AMC factory in Plumstead. When AMC collapsed, Manganese Bronze Holdings took over and focused their attention on the Atlas engine and designed a new frame, the 'Isolastic' system, which isolated engine vibration from the main frame.

In 1972 Norton-Villiers took over the ailing Triumph-BSA company, but due to factory disputes and disrupted production the entire motorcycle production ceased. Fortunately the Norton name was retained and a new division was set up at Andover – Norton Motors (1978).

1914/1916 Norton 490cc, in good condition throughout, with buff log book.
£5,800–6,200 *S*

By the time that this machine was built Norton were producing engines of their own, in both 633cc and 490cc versions.

NEW IMPERIAL *(British)*

1934 New Imperial Model 40, finished with black frame and cycle parts, chromium plated petrol tank, complete and in good condition.
£850–1,000 *S*

NORMAN *(British)*

1957 Norman Villiers 80, 4 speed gearbox, requires repainting.
£650–800 *CBr*

1929 Norton Model 18 500cc, fully restored, twin barrel silencer and cast aluminium primary chain casing, old and new style registration documents.
£6,700–7,000 *S*

The new Model 18 for 1929 featured the stylish saddle tank, and not only was it good looking, it had performance and renowned Norton handling to match.

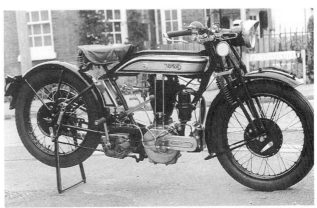

1926 Norton Model 18 500cc.
£7,500–8,500 *AtMC*

1929 500cc Norton CS1 Overhead Camshaft.
£9,000–10,000 *AtMC*

1932 Norton Model 40 International Racer,
with classic overhead camshaft engine and 4 speed
Sturmey Archer gearbox, no modifications to
catalogue specification, excellent condition.
£4,500–5,500 *S*

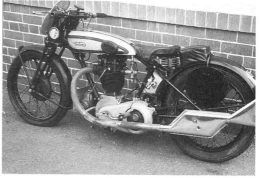

1930 Norton Model 18 500cc.
£2,500–3,500 *WCM*

1936/1938 Works International 'Manx'
Specification Norton, excellent condition.
Est. £11,000–13,000 *S*

*This machine features the specially lightened
frame introduced for the 1936 season featuring
plunger rear suspension with lightening holes
applied, leading to the pepperpot nickname.
Only two other examples of this rare model are
known to survive.*

1939/1947 Norton Manx 30M 498cc Motorcycle,
dohc cylinder head, 1939 Inter crankcases, engine
rebuilt, clutch cable, foot rest rubbers and
handlebar grips.
Est. £11,500–12,000 *S*

c1939 Norton 16H Solo, good
overall condition.
£1,500–2,000 *S*

1948 Norton Model 18 500cc.
£2,000–3,000 *WCM*

1948 Norton International.
£7,000–7,500 *AtMC*

1948 Norton Big Four 633cc.
£1,500–1,800 *BCB*

1949 Norton Model 30 International 490cc,
excellent condition, well documented history.
Est. £20,000–25,000 *S*

1949 Norton ES2 500cc, finished in
Norton's traditional black and silver livery,
good condition throughout.
£1,900–2,300 *S*

1951 Norton 500cc T Trials, finished in
silver with a black frame and polished alloy
mudguards, very good condition.
Est. £3,500–4,500 *S*

1951 Norton ES2 500cc.
£3,000–3,500 *AtMC*

1952 Norton Manx Model 40, later twin leading
shoe front brake, new rear hub to the correct
specification, good condition throughout.
Est. £9,000–12,000 *S*

This excellent example of Norton's 40M Manx was
originally supplied by the factory to a member of the
RAF serving in Singapore.

1953 Norton Manx 30M 499cc Single Cylinder
Solo Racer, rebuilt throughout to a very high
standard, fitted with a works front end, with
doubled anchor twin leading shoe front brake.
£25,000–27,000 *S*

1953 Norton 500 T Trials.
£3,000–3,500 *AtMC*

1954 Norton Manx Short Stroke 'Double Knocker' Overhead Camshaft 350cc.
£15,000–16,000 *CBr*
A classic racing bike.

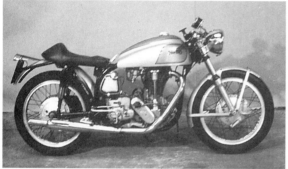

c1957 Norton International Special 500cc,
Inter engine and featherbed frame with later pattern front forks, Goldie pattern silencer, finished in black and silver with red lining and polished alloy, good condition mechanically.
Est. £4,200–4,400 *S*

1957 Norton Model 195 597cc,
finished in silver and black to a high standard, 'pear' shaped silencer, believed to be to catalogue specification.
Est. £2,200–2,600 *S*

1957 Norton Model 19S 600cc, finished in traditional silver and black, fully restored to a high standard throughout.
£2,900–3,200 *S*

1957/1958 Norton Manx 350cc,
original frame and tyres, rebuilt magneto, very good condition.
Est. £8,000–10,000 *S*

This machine was purchased in 1964 as a Ray Petty 250, but the engine blew up the following year. It was then fitted with a Bill Stuart tuned 350cc engine, and in this guise the vendor raced it with some success at short circuits and in the TT. In the last season in which it raced, in 1969, the machine earned its rider a bronze medal in the Junior TT.

> **Miller's is a price GUIDE not a price LIST**

1958 Norton 350cc.
£1,150–1,300 *PS*

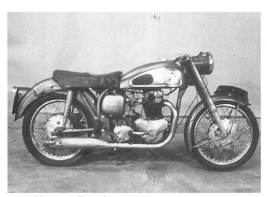

1958 Norton Manx 350cc.
£11,000–12,500 *AtMC*

1958 Norton Dominator 88 500cc, finished
in silver and grey, original condition.
£2,600–3,000 *S*

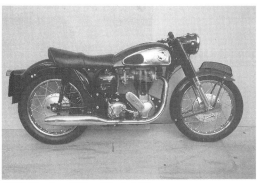

1958 Norton Dominator 88 500cc,
excellent condition.
£2,600–3,000 *S*

1959 Norton 30 M Manx 499cc Racer, traditional
Norton livery of silver, red and black, white fairing,
very good mechanical condition, fitted with Quaife
5 speed gearbox and Grimeca front brake.
Est. £10,000–11,000 *S*

*Norton's classic racing Manx is an original 500cc
Manx racer used from 1970 until 1991 by Will
Collard in classic racing.*

1960 Norton 350cc Model 50.
£3,200–3,700 *VER*

1961 Norton Dunstall 99SS.
£2,500–2,900 *VER*

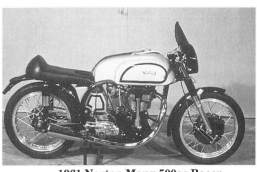

1961 Norton 99 600cc Café Racer, rebuilt.
Est. £3,000–3,500 *S*

1961 Norton Manx 500cc Racer,
'double knocker' twin overhead camshaft,
excellent condition throughout.
Est. £14,000–16,000 *S*

1962 Norton SS 650, finished in black and silver, unrestored and in good original condition.
Est. £3,500–4,000 *HOLL*

1964 Norton Dominator 88SS 500cc.
£2,200–3,000 *WCM*

1969 Norton Commando Fastback Overhead Valve 750cc, finished in black, excellent condition both mechanically and cosmetically.
Est. £4,000–5,000 *S*

1970 Norton Norvil 750cc Racer, single seat conversion, half fairing, twin high level exhausts fitted with megaphones and single disc brake, finished in traditional Norton racing colours of silver with red and black pinstriping, excellent condition throughout.
Est. £4,000–5,000 *S*

1974 Norton Commando 850cc, average original condition, low mileage.
£2,300–2,600 *S*

This example of the Norton Commando has seen service with the RAF Military Police and is still in police livery.

1977 Norton Commando Mk III, finished in black, good original condition.
Est. £2,500–3,000 *LF*

These big twins were repeatedly voted the best British twin in magazine reader surveys.

> **Miller's is a price GUIDE not a price LIST**

1968 Norton Atlas 750cc Twin Cylinder Overhead Valve 4 Stroke, finished in red, good condition throughout, rebuilt.
£3,300–3,500 *S*

NSU *(German)*

1934 NSU 500cc Overhead Camshaft.
£17,000–20,000 *AtMC*

OEC *(British)*

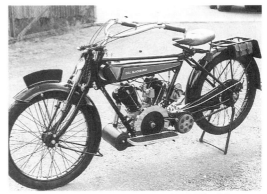

1922 OEC Blackburne.
£8,000–9,000 *AtMC*

OK *(British)*

Humphries & Dawes Ltd., of Hall Green,
Birmingham, were among the very earliest of
British motorcycle manufacturers,
commencing production in 1899. Their OK
machines, later remembered under the OK
Supreme name, were made with a variety of
power units, including their own engines, such
as their 292cc 2 stroke, and Blackburne 247cc
and 347cc sv and ohv engines.

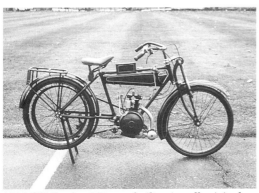

1924 OK Junior 269cc, rebuilt using all original
parts, in good condition throughout.
£1,600–2,000 *S*

*This machine is typical of the lightweights built by
the firm under the Junior model name. Powered by
a Villiers 2 stroke engine with a single speed and
belt drive.*

1927 OK Supreme 250cc.
£3,200–3,700 *AtMC*

OSSA *(Spanish)*

1972 OSSA 250cc Trials, twin shock series.
£850–950 *CBr*

PANTHER (P & M) *(British)*

Phelon & Moore started production of their P & M machines in Yorkshire in 1900, and the company continued to build machines until 1965. The title P & M was gradually dropped in favour of the name Panther, and all bikers will be aware of the slopers which typified the marque. In the 1930s, however, the company built a range of Villiers engined 2 strokes, known as Red Panthers, specifically for the London dealers Pride & Clarke.

1935 P & M Red Panther 250cc, 3 speed hand gear change, very good condition throughout.
£1,200–1,500 *LF*

1916 P & M 3½hp 500cc.
£2,000–2,200 *LF*

1936 Red Panther 250cc, good mechanical and cosmetic condition.
£1,200–1,500 *S*

PEUGEOT *(French)*

1929 Peugeot P107 350cc, long wheelbase, side valve, engine and 3 speed hand change gearbox, overhauled in 1990.
£2,600–3,000 *S*

RALEIGH *(British)*

Raleigh's entry into the world of motorcycle production got off to a bumpy start. In 1902 they manufactured their first bike, a copy of the Werner Motocyclette, but production ceased in 1905. It was not until 1919 that Raleigh re-entered the market with a new 650cc flat twin.

1922 Raleigh 350cc Solo.
£1,800–2,100 *LW*

PRAGA *(Czechoslovakian)*

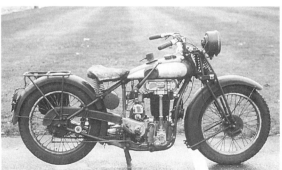

c1930 Praga 350cc, military green, running order.
Est. £3,500–4,000 *S*

1924 Raleigh No. 5 2½hp Solo, fitted with a period Cowey speedometer, and Powell and Hammer acetylene lighting set.
Est. £4,000–6,000 *S*

This Raleigh was restored in 1983 and has documented evidence to show it won many concours awards for both Vintage and Best in Show. The machine was also the winner of the Banbury run Class B in 1985.

1925 Raleigh 3 Horse Power Solo.
£3,000–3,500 *LW*

1925 Raleigh Model 5 350cc, total restoration, fitted with Sturmey Archer 3 speed gearbox, luggage carrier and wicker basket, full acetylene lighting set and leather tool carrier, concours condition, with old log book, excellent condition throughout.
£4,000–4,500 *S*

1926 Raleigh 798cc Twin Cylinder Solo.
£4,800–5,300 *LW*

1928 Raleigh 250cc Touring, rebuilt, with girder forks, rigid frame at the rear and 3 speed hand change gearbox, good condition.
Est. £1,900–2,000 *S*

1928 Raleigh 250cc, fitted with Sturmey Archer engine and 3 speed gearbox, totally restored, concours condition throughout, fitted with luggage carrier, stand and leather toolbox.
£3,400–3,800 *S*

1928 Raleigh Model 23 500cc, finished in black livery, in good condition to original specification.
£3,800–4,300 *S*

1930 Raleigh MA30 496cc, finished in black and cream, very good condition throughout.
£2,000–2,500 *S*

This is one of only five remaining examples of Raleigh's side valve 496cc 3 speed model MA30.

1931 Raleigh 500cc Solo, 3 speed hand change gearbox, original specification.
£2,400–2,800 *S*

1933 Raleigh 598cc Solo.
£1,150–1,300 *LW*

ROYAL ENFIELD
(British 1901–70, Indian 1950s)

Royal Enfield experimented with motorcycle engines in 1901, but it was not until 1911 that they offered their first motorcycle for sale, a 425cc MAG V-twin. From 1912 to 1920 they produced a variety of bikes but not until 1920 did they produced their own engines. By the late 1920s only RE engines were used in all their designs.

RE specialised in a collection of bikes that were initially manufactured for export, such as the luxurious 1140cc side valve V-twin and the 125cc copy of the DKW 2 stroke, and much later (1967) the Interceptor twin was made for export to the US. During the 1940s and 1950s RE produced their most popular bikes the Bullet series, the 700cc Meteor twin and Crusader.

In 1963 the company was sold to E. & H. P. Smith engineering group but shortly thereafter a rapid decline in British sales led to cut backs of the range and the company was again sold to NVT at Bradford-on-Avon. Although the Royal Enfield marque ceased production in the UK in 1970, Enfield India Ltd., a branch of Royal Enfield, established in Madras in the 1950s to concentrate on 173cc production and other small machines, continues to manufacture and export the 346cc and 499cc Bullet models.

RAYMO (French)

The Desmailles Brothers controlled the production of Raymo motorcycles which formed part of a company selling bicycles and furniture in Ain, France. In 1923 they began building their own lightweight machines which followed on to larger motorcycles using Blackburne engines in 1928, and Moser and Voisin engines in 1929.

1930 Raymo Type R11 350cc Sports, good condition, full restoration, new tyres.
Est. £4,200–4,500 *S*

RICKMAN (British)

1974 Rickman Zündapp, formerly used by the police.
£750–900 *CBr*

1921 Royal Enfield 2½hp Solo, original paintwork and transfers, original leather saddle, coffee grinder gear change, P & H acetylene headlamp, 'tower' rear lamp, leg shields and luggage carrier, V-handlebars.
Est. £1,700–2,000 *S*

1923 Royal Enfield VT 1000cc.
£6,500–7,000 *AtMc*

1924 Royal Enfield 350cc Sports, finished in traditional livery of black frame with green and yellow tank and red logo, good condition throughout.
Est. £2,000–2,400 *S*

1926 Royal Enfield 3.46hp Standard Model 350, 3 speed Sturmey Archer gearbox, hand operated clutch and kickstart, mechanical pump and supplementary hand operated pump, acetylene front and rear lamps, luggage carrier with leather panniers and period nickel RAC ACU badge, restored to high standard, old style log book.
£3,500–4,000 *S*

1931 Royal Enfield Model K 976cc, 3 speed hand change gearbox, rigid frame at rear and coil spring and girder forks, good condition throughout, original fittings.
£1,700–2,000 *S*

1934 Royal Enfield Model T Overhead Valve Single Cylinder Model 143cc, fully enclosed valve gear, 4 speed gearbox, original buff log book.
£800–1,000 *PS*

1953 Royal Enfield RAF Solo, requires restoration.
£70–100 *S*

1954 Royal Enfield Bullet 346cc Trials, factory built model, reconditioned, good condition.
£2,700–3,000 *S*

- In 1926 Royal Enfield offered both a side valve and overhead valve version of their 3.46hp, 346cc model.
- The lightweight 125cc two stroke was popular with the RAF.
- The Bullet was very successful in trials competition during the 1950s before it was superceded by the lighter Crusader in 1957.

1955 Royal Enfield Bullet 346cc.
£800–1,000 *LF*

1960 Royal Enfield Crusader Sports 248cc, complete, needs restoration, original buff log book.
£500–800 *S*

One of the most popular derivatives was the Crusader Sports which featured dropped handlebars, reverse mounted footrests, a light alloy cylinder head, 8.5:1 compression ratio, hotter cams and a larger carburettor. The result could exceed 80mph and still return 92mpg, under normal condtions.

1963 Royal Enfield Overhead Valve Single Cylinder Model 248cc, new engine bearings, rebore, new piston, completely rebuilt, very good condition, original buff logbook.
£450–800 *PS*

1968 Royal Enfield Crusader Sports Overhead Valve Single Cylinder Model 248cc, original condition, requires restoration.
£800–1,100 *PS*

1970 Royal Enfield Interceptor Series II 736cc, 4 speed gearbox with neutral finder, finished in black, chrome and red livery, original electrical equipment.
Est. £4,000–4,500 *S*

1962 Royal Enfield 248cc Trials.
£1,700–2,000 *PS*

1967 Royal Enfield Interceptor Series 1 736cc, parallel twin cylinder engine, renewed black and blue paintwork, completely rebuilt.
£2,700–3,000 *S*

ROYAL RUBY *(British)*

1919 Royal Ruby 2 Stroke Single Cylinder Model 269cc, early Villiers design engine, new beaded edge tyres, totally original and complete.
£1,300–1,800 *PS*

RUDGE *(British)*

1929 Rudge Whitworth 250cc Twin Port, mechanically rebuilt, repainted in correct black with gold livery.
Est. £2,000–3,000 *S*

Only a small amount of work is needed to complete the restoration of this bike, with only the headlight, silencers and other small parts needing to be fitted.

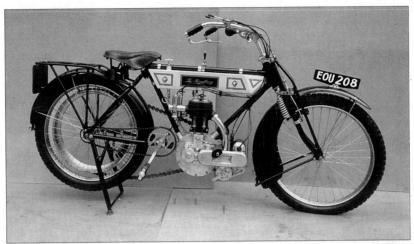

1922 Rudge Multi 500cc,
rebuilt to original specification,
excellent condition.
£3,000–3,500 *S*

c1923 Rudge Multi 500cc.
£7,000–7,500 *AtMC*

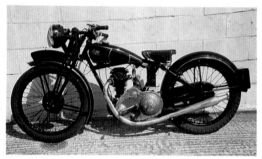

1931 Rudge 250 Overhead Valve.
£2,400–2,800 *AT*

1937 Rudge Ulster 500cc, racing trim.
£2,000–2,500 *BCB*

1937 Rudge Rapid 250cc.
£4,000–4,500 *AtMC*

c1938 Rudge Ulster 500cc.
£4,500–5,000 *AtMC*

1939 Rudge Ulster 500cc.
£4,500–5,000 *VER*

1939 Rudge Rapid 250cc, overhead valve,
alloy cylinder head, centre stand operated by
hand lever.
£2,300–2,800 *RJES*

1927 Scott Flying Squirrel 600cc,
2 speed gearbox.
£4,500–5,000 *AtMC*

1926 Scott Flying Squirrel 600cc, water cooled,
twin cylinders, 2 stroke engine, 2 speed gearbox.
£3,500–4,200 *BCB*

c1927 Scott Flying Squirrel 2 speed.
£4,000–5,000 *AtMC*

1928 Scott Flying Squirrel 600cc, water
cooled twin.
£3,500–4,000 *BCB*

1968 Seeley G50 Mk2 500cc.
£16,000–17,000 *AtMC*

1938 Simplex, in American Air Force livery.
£500–750 *CBr*

1968 Suzuki T20C 250cc Street Scrambler,
high level exhaust system.
Est. £2,400–3,000 *S*

A very rare version of the T20 Super Six.

1966 Sprite 37A engine, round barrel, original
lighting, good condition.
£950–1,100 *CBr*

1979 Suzuki RG500 Mk4.
£4,500–5,000 *AtMC*

1912 Sunbeam 500cc.
£6,000–7,000 *AtMC*

1915 Sunbeam 3½hp 500cc.
£4,800–6,000 *AT*

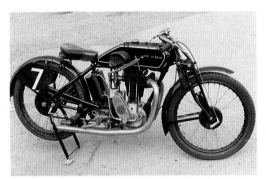

1925 Sunbeam 90 500cc, Brooklands racer.
£6,800–7,500 *AtMC*

1916 Sunbeam MAG, Swiss engine V-twin.
£7,800–9,000 *AtMC*
Mainly sold to the Russian Army during WWI.

1930 Sunbeam Model 9 500cc.
£4,600–5,000 *VER*

1927 Sunbeam Model 8 350cc.
£4,200–4,900 *AtMC*

1928 Sunbeam Model 7 600cc.
£4,500–5,000 *AtMC*

1932 Sunbeam Model 9S 493cc, rebuilt,
very good condition.
£3,800–4,300 *S*

1934 Sunbeam Long Stroke Lion Sports 492cc, mechanically very good, complete, original condition.
Est. £6,000–6,500 *S*

1934 Sunbeam 250.
£4,000–4,800 *AtMC*

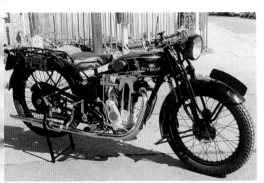

1935 Sunbeam Model 9 500cc.
£4,000–4,500 *AtMC*

1936 Sunbeam Lion 500cc.
£3,000–3,500 *AtMC*

1935 Sunbeam Model 9.
£4,000–4,500 *AtMC*

1938 Sunbeam Model 9 Solo, with valanced mudguards, original buff logbook.
£2,200–2,800 *S*

1950 Sunbeam S8 487cc, single overhead cam twin, 12 volt electrical system, original log book.
£3,800–4,200 *S*

1952 Sunbeam S8 500cc, shaft drive overhead cam in line, all aluminium.
£2,000–2,500 *BCB*

1950 Sunbeam S7 500cc.
£3,500–4,000 *VER*

1958 Triton 650cc, pre-unit engine, wide line frame, restored.
£2,500–3,000 *BCB*

1958 Triton 650cc, pre-unit engine, wide line frame, rebuilt.
£2,700–3,000 *BCB*

c1960 Triton T110 650cc Solo Café Racer, overhead valve 4 stroke, Triumph slickshift gearbox, Norton telescopic roadholder forks, pivoted rear suspension, hand built special.
£2,250–2,500 *OxM*

c1960 Triton A.R.E. 750cc Solo Café Racer, overhead valve 4 stroke, pivoted fork rear suspension, Grimeca 4LS front brake, Norton Featherbed wideline frame, hand built special.
£2,800–3,300 *OxM*

1962 Triton 750cc Solo Café Racer, vertical twin, overhead valve 4 stroke, Triumph gearbox, Norton telescopic roadholder forks, pivoted fork rear suspension, TLS front brake, hand built special. **£2,250–2,500** *OxM*

1962 Triton T120R 650cc, wideline frame.
£3,500–4,300 *WCM*

1962 Triton TR6 650cc Solo Café Racer, overhead valve 4 stroke, Norton telescopic roadholder forks, pivoted fork rear suspension, hand built special. **£1,800–2,200** *OxM*

1964 Triton 650cc Solo Café Racer, overhead valve 4 stroke, Triumph gearbox, Norton Featherbed slimline frame, hand built special.
£1,500–1,800 *OxM*

1914 Triumph 500cc.
£4,500–5,000 *VER*

c1925 Triumph SD 500cc.
£4,500–5,000 *AtMC*

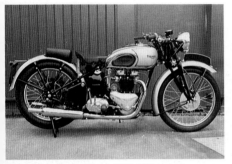

1938 Triumph Tiger 100 498cc, twin
cylinder, restored.
£4,750–5,500 *HH*

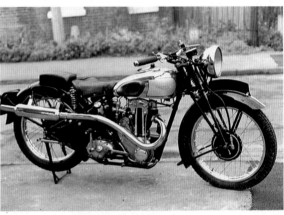

c1938 Triumph Tiger 70.
£3,500–4,250 *AtMC*

1938 Triumph Tiger 80 350cc.
£3,500–4,500 *WCM*

c1938 Triumph Spread Twin 500cc.
£4,500–5,000 *AtMC*

1949 Triumph Trophy TR5 498cc, twin
cylinder, Generator Unit/Grand Prix cylinder
barrel and head.
£5,750–6,150 *HH*

Top **1953 Triumph 6T 650cc.**
Bottom **1950 Triumph Thunderbird 6T 650cc.**
£2,000–2,500 **each** *PM*

1950 Triumph Thunderbird 650cc, restored.
£3,000–3,300 *BCB*

1952 Triumph Thunderbird 649cc, twin
cylinder, very good restored condition.
£3,150–4,000 *HH*

1953 Triumph Speed Twin 500cc,
good original condition.
£1,800–2,200 *MR*

1955 Triumph 150 Terrier.
£800–1,500 *WCM*

1956 Triumph TR6 Trophy 650cc, twin
cylinder sports, version of pre-unit separate
gearbox engine, single carburettor, two-into-one
high mounted Siamese exhaust system, single
sided front hub brake. **£6,000–6,500** *HC*

1957 Triumph T110.
£4,800–5,250 *VER*

1957 Tiger Cub Special.
£1,200–1,400 *PM*

1957 Triumph Thunderbird 6T 650cc.
£2,000–2,500 *PM*

1958 Triumph T100 500cc, with optional twin carburettors, splayed head.
£3,000–4,000 *WCM*

1958 Triumph 650 Thunderbird.
£3,500–4,500 *WCM*

1958 Triumph Trophy TR6 649cc, twin cylinders, US version.
£5,500–6,000 *HH*

1959 Triumph T120 650cc.
£6,000–6,500 *AtMC*

1960 Triumph Tiger T110 Bathtub 650cc, UK specification, original condition.
£2,500–3,500 *GLC*

1960 Triumph TR6 Trophy 650cc, single carburettor, completely rebuilt.
£4,250–4,600 *AT*

1961 Triumph T120 Bonneville 649cc, twin cylinders, twin carburettor, restored.
£4,500–5,750 *HH*

1965 Triumph Tiger 90 3TA 350cc.
£1,500–1,900 *PM*

1964 Triumph T100SS 500cc, restored.
£2,200–2,600 *BCB*

1969 Triumph Bonneville 650cc.
£3,500–4,000 *S*

1969 Triumph T120 Bonneville 650cc, twin carburettors, restored.
£3,250–3,500 *BCB*

1970 Triumph T120 Bonneville 650cc, Coni rear shocks, UK specification.
£3,000–4,000 *GLC*

1969 Triumph TR6 Trophy.
£2,400–3,400 *WCM*

1970 Triumph Bonneville 650cc.
£3,200–3,500 *BCB*

1972 Triumph Bonneville T120 650cc, 4 speed, US specification.
£2,800–3,500 *GLC*

1971 Triumph TR6 Trophy 650cc, single carburettor, US specification.
£2,500–3,000 *BCB*

1977 Triumph Bonneville Jubilee 750cc.
£3,000–3,500 *AtMC*

1978 Triumph Bonneville T140V 750cc, 5 speed, original Norton silencers, UK specification.
£2,500–3,500 *GLC*

1933 Velocette KTS 350cc.
£5,000–5,500 *AtMC*

1934 Velocette MOV 250cc.
£3,400–3,700 *AtMC*

c1937 Velocette KSS MkII.
£5,000–5,500 *AtMC*

1937 Velocette MSS 495cc Solo, rebuilt,
good condition.
£2,100–2,500 *S*

1941 Velocette KSS MkII 350cc, post-
war Dowty forks, very good condition.
£2,800–3,200 *S*

c1948 Velocette MkVIII.
£14,000–16,000 *AtMC*

1939 Velocette GTP 250cc.
£2,000–2,500 *VER*

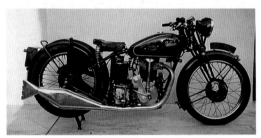

1949 Velocette KSS 350cc, overhead camshaft.
£4,250–4,750 *VER*

1948 Velocette KTT 350cc MkVIII Racer,
engine rebuilt, restored, very good condition.
Est. £16,000–20,000 *BKS*

1950 Velocette MAC 350cc.
£1,800–2,000 *PM*

1950 Velocette MAC 350cc.
£2,600–3,000 *VER*

1955 Velocette MSS 500cc.
£3,000–3,500 *AtMC*

1956 Velocette Venom 500cc.
£3,500–4,000 *VER*

1958 Velocette Valiant 200cc solo, restored,
excellent condition throughout.
£1,100–1,400 *S*

1959 Velocette LE 200cc, water-cooled
horizontally opposed twin, completely restored.
£1,100–1,300 *S*

1961 Velocette Venom 500cc.
£3,000–4,000 *BCB*

1964 Velocette Venom 500cc, restored to
concours standard.
£4,500–5,000 *BCB*

1962 Velocette Venom Clubman.
£8,500–9,200 *AtMC*

1964 Velocette LE 200cc.
£650–800 *PM*

**1964 Velocette Viper Vee Line Special
349cc,** engine rebuilt, rewired, good condition.
£2,400–2,800 *S*

1921 Verus, 4 stroke, belt drive, rebuilt, good condition.
£1,800–2,200 *HOLL*

1977 Yamaha RD 250cc, 350 miles from new, excellent condition.
£1,400–1,600 *S*

1974 Yamaha TY 250A Trials, good condition throughout.
£550–650 *S*

1976 Yamaha TZ700 Square-Four 700cc, restored, excellent condition.
£9,000–10,000 *BKS*

1923 Zenith Gradua.
£9,000–10,000 *AtMC*

c1953 NSU Quickly Moped 50cc, original condition.
£180–200 *S*

1924 Zenith Blackburne.
£35,000–40,000 *AtMC*

1960 NSU Prima 150cc Motor Scooter, good condition throughout.
£600–800 *S*

1952 BSA A10 Gordon Flash, plunger frame.
£2,500–3,000 *RCMC*

1950 BSA A10 650cc, fitted with a Watsonian
Palma sports sidecar combination, restored,
good condition.
£2,700–3,000 *S*

**c1958 BSA Gold Star 499cc Works
Supported Trials combination,**
restored, in good condition.
Est. £5,000–7,000 *S*

c1955 Watsonian Avon Replica Sidecar,
fitted to a Norton.
£1,500–2,000 excluding bike *CCR*

1936 OEC JAP.
£9,000–10,000 *AtMC*

1956 Norton 19S 600cc and Stein Sidecar,
restored throughout, excellent condition.
Est. £4,000–6,000 *S*

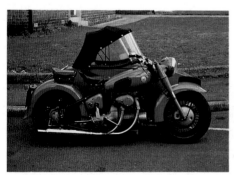

**1951 Sunbeam 500 S8 with Watsonian
Monarch Single Seater.**
£3,000–3,500 *PM*

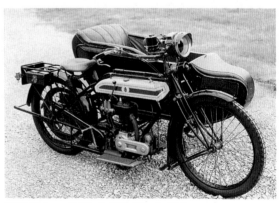

1923 Triumph Model H, Gloria Sidecar.
£6,500–7,000 *AtMC*

1927 Triumph 50 550cc.
£5,000–5,750 *VER*

1953 Triumph T100 and STE1B sidecar.
£6,500–7,000 *AtMC*

1961 Triumph T120R 650cc.
£4,000–4,500 *PM*

1952 Vincent
Rapide Series C
1,000cc and
Swallow Jet 80
Sidecar, restored,
very good condition.
£11,500–12,500
BKS

1950 Garrard GP sidecar, fitted to Vincent
1000cc, rebuilt using stainless steel.
£2,500–3,000 *CCR*

1963 Watsonian Monza sidecar,
very good condition.
£900–1,000 *CCR*

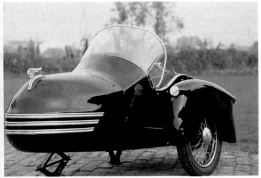

c1950 Watsonian Monaco MkI Sidecar, rebuilt.
£1,500–2,000 *CCR*

1942 Zündapp KS750, 170° overhead valve
V-twin, reverse gear, sidecar wheel drive through
a differential.
£6,000–7,000 *MVT*

A Butlins Motorcycle Club Badge, 1950–60s.
£50–60 *MCh*

1930s Triumph Cycles Agency Sign.
£80–90 *PMB*

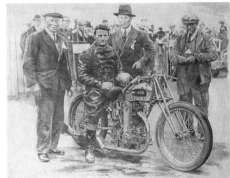

Bert Denley, original watercolour artwork of AJS works racing team, c1928.
£750–850 *MCh*

A selection of WWII motorcyclist's clothing, comprising: leather coat, hood, boots, goggles and a pair of gauntlets.
£400–450 *HOLL*

A Motorcycle Medallion, one of a set of seven, c1928.
£200–250 *BCA*

A Shell Lubricating Oil Can.
£20–30 *PMB*

A James Cycles and Motorcycles Sign, c1920.
£130–150 *PMB*

A B.S.A. Motorcycle Sign, c1930.
£150–200 *PMB*

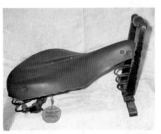

A Sprung Leather Motorcycle Saddle, c1920, suitable for various machines.
£10–15 *PC*

A Wills's Star Cigarettes Advertising Board, c1937.
£400–500 *PMB*

SCOTT *(British)*

Affectionately known as 'The Yowling Two-Stroke', the Scott is one of the most idiosyncratic of all British bikes. They demand to be noticed, and generate a love/hate relationship unique to the marque. Yorkshireman Alfred Scott produced his first machine in 1908. Characteristic of the early machines was the petrol drum beneath the saddle and a kickstarter. During the 1920s and 30s the twin cylinder water-cooled 2 stroke machines performed well in TT events and off road events. Despite these successes, sales were dropping and the company was eventually sold to Matt Holder in 1950. Attempts to modernise the Scott's appearance were in vain and production ceased in the late 1960s.

1928 Scott 596cc TT Replica, very good condition throughout.
£3,500–3,800 *S*

c1927 Scott Flyer 498cc TT Replica, with 1927 engine, 3 speed gearbox, new radiator to original pattern, black and scarlet paintwork, black leatherette seat, mechanically good, electric lighting.
£3,600–3,800 *S*

1930 Scott Squirrel Super Sports, good mechanical and cosmetic condition.
£3,300–3,700 *S*

1930 Scott Flying Squirrel Deluxe, hand operated gear change, very good condition.
£2,900–3,500 *LF*

1931 Scott Squirrel 500cc, black and ivory, good condition.
£4,200–4,800 *S*

1950 Scott Springer Flying Squirrel 596cc, electrics feature a serviced pancake dynamo and connect system, finished in original black stove enamel.
£2,000–2,500 *S*

This historic machine is the last prototype Scott built at Shipley before the original Scott works went bankrupt. Intended for the 1951 season, this spring frame model proved too expensive to make, given the competition in the market from other manufacturers at that time.

1931 Scott 498cc, finished in black and purple, good condition.
£2,500–3,500 *S*

1958 Scott Swift 500cc, 3 speed gearbox, black and chrome livery, original electrical equipment, very good condition.
Est. £4,500–5,000 *S*

This machine features Scott twin points coil ignition, and a specially tuned Swift engine. Further evolution of the Scott engine was halted when the Scott works were the subject of a compulsory purchase order.

1958 Scott Swift 500cc, Swift engine, flat top pistons, twin monoblocs, 3 speed gearbox, black and chrome, original electrical equipment.
£3,500–4,000 *S*

SUNBEAM *(British)*

As with many successful motorcycle marques, Sunbeam was first made by bicycle makers John Marston. Initially they made a 350cc single cylinder and later a 500cc side valve single which established Sunbeam's reputation as a serious motorcycle concern and winner of several TT races. Success followed the company until the Depression of the 1930s set in, their sales deteriorated and Sunbeam was sold to Nobel Industries (now ICI) and then five years later it was sold again to AMC.

AMC moved production to London where the 250cc, 350cc and 500cc models were produced. Scarcely had these bikes reached the showroom when, during WWII, Sunbeam was sold to BSA. Under BSA control, Sunbeam produced the S7 and S8 models, neither of which reached the sales levels anticipated by BSA. In 1957 Sunbeam production ended and the name was used on bicycles.

SINGER *(British)*

1901 Singer 208cc Solo, black livery with dull nickel fittings, original, period Phillips rope sprung saddle, acetylene cycle headlamp, bugle horn, fuel tank slung from the crossbar bearing the royal VR monogram.
£6,500–7,000 *S*

Singer & Co. Ltd. of Coventry commenced production with a tri-car before launching their first motorcycle which was essentially a heavy duty bicycle fitted with a Perks & Birch Motorised Wheel.

1928 Sunbeam Model 8 350cc, original unrestored condition.
Est. £3,250–3,750 *S*

1929 Sunbeam Longstroke 492cc, black paintwork, good condition throughout.
Est. £3,000–4,000 *S*

1929 Sunbeam Model 8 350cc, finished in traditional black and gold livery, good condition throughout, fitted with straight through exhaust system, features the newly introduced saddle tank.
£3,000–3,500 *S*

Although dating from the year following Sunbeam's takeover by ICI, this example of the 350cc overhead valve Model 8 demonstrates the design integrity and quality for which the John Marston built Vintage Sunbeams are renowned.

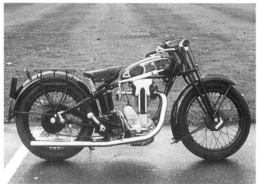

1933 Sunbeam Model 9 500cc,
cosmetically excellent, rebuilt, features
the saddle tank and fishtail exhaust.
£2,800–3,000 *S*

1933 Sunbeam Model 9 600cc,
overhead valve single cylinder engine,
excellent original condition throughout,
electric lighting set, leather tool boxes,
old style log book.
£4,300–4,800 *S*

1934 Sunbeam Model 90 500cc.
£4,500–5,000 *AtMC*

1939 Sunbeam Model B25 500cc Solo,
chain driven high camshaft, hairpin valve
springs, very good condition.
£4,200–4,600 *S*

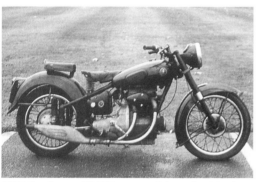

1949 Sunbeam S8 500cc, complete and original,
needs restoration.
£1,000–1,200 *S*

- Sunbeam's vintage products earned an outstanding reputation for high quality finish and engineering.
- Introduced in 1949, the S8 was developed from the S7 overhead cam twin cylinder tourer.

1952 Sunbeam S8, finished in black,
rebuilt, 4 speed foot change, excellent
condition throughout.
Est. £2,000–2,500 *LF*

SUZUKI *(Japanese)*

Although Suzuki produced motorised bicycles in 1952 it was not until 1955 that they produced their first motorcycle, the 125cc 2 stroke Colleda. During the early 1960s Suzuki won numerous TT races in the 50cc and 125cc classes before withdrawing from Grand Prix racing in 1965. In motocross racing they experienced even more success with their single cycliner 2 strokes during the 1960s and 70s.

As well as winning races, the market for Suzuki road bikes was equally astonishing. They claimed to be the world's largest maker of 2 strokes and exported a large proportion of their bikes to the US. In the late 70s they introduced a new generation of 4 stroke fours and twins which sold well.

1975 Suzuki TR750 Works Solo Racer, excellent original condition.
£17,300–18,000 *S*

This machine was campaigned by Barry Sheene during the 1975/76 seasons for Suzuki GB and Heron Suzuki before passing to Steve Parrish towards the end of 1976. During 1977 it would appear that it was used by Percy Tait in his capacity as a support rider. This would indicate that this machine, or Barry Sheene's, took first places in France, Sweden and Britain during the 1975 Formula 750 series.

1974 Suzuki TR 500cc Solo Racer, restored to original condition.
Est. £16,000–17,000 *S*

This example of Suzuki's twin cylinder 2 stroke machine was raced by Barry Sheene for the Suzuki GB team prior to the introduction of the 4 cylinder machines.

1975 Heron-Suzuki TR750 3 Cylinder Racer, completely restored.
£25,500+ *BKS*

This machine, one of a pair imported into the UK in the Spring of 1975, was campaigned by Barry Sheene in the Formula 750 series, competing at Mettet, Assen, Silverstone and winning at Anderstorp in Sweden.

1977 Suzuki GT250, with disc front brake.
£100–200 *S*

c1979 Suzuki TS250 Vic Camp Racer, good condition.
£100–150 *S*

1976 Suzuki GT380, 3 cylinder 2 stroke, 6 speed gearbox, original condition.
£1,500–1,600 *S*

TANDON *(British)*

1954 Tandon 150cc Competition Scrambler, pivoted fork rear suspension and Earles type forks, original condition.
Est. £600–800 *S*

The Tandon concern was established in 1948 with the aim of building cheap lightweights, however the company soon branched out into competition machines featuring a rubber controlled rear suspension system. This is an ex-works machine used by H. E. J. Babb, introduced in 1953.

TORPEDO *(British)*

1912 Torpedo 212cc, precision powered, belt driven, acetylene headlight, unrestored but complete.
Est. £2,750–3,000 *S*

There were a number of unrelated motorcycle makers who sold bikes under the Torpedo name. This example was made by F. Hopper & Co. Ltd., of Barton on Humber, Lincolnshire, who were in business from 1910 until 1920, later being associated with Elswick Hopper pedal cycles. They used Precision engines up to 500cc.

TRITON *(British)*

The first Triton was built in 1954 by 'inventor' Doug Clarke from a Triumph T110 engine and Norton featherbed frame. This combination provided the speed and reliability of the Triumph engine and the ease of handling of the Norton frame. So popular was this union that a Triton Owners Club was established and today boasts a membership of over 200 members.

**1957 Triton T100 500cc.
£2,500–3,500** *WCM*

1956 Triton Club Racer T110, wideline frame.
£2,000–3,000 *WCM*

1960 Triton 650cc, Norton Featherbed frame, Norton Manx front brake, Triumph twin engine, alloy tank and wheels, full lighting equipment.
£2,600–2,800 *PC*

**1959 Triton 650.
£3,800–4,000** *LF*

1963 Triton 650 T120R, slimline frame.
£2,000–3,500 *WCM*

1968 Dresda Triton 650cc Twin Cylinder Overhead Valve 4 Stroke, Tiger 110 engine, swept back exhausts with Goldie type silencers, exposed fork and rear shock absorber springs, central oil tank clip-ons and rear sets, completely rebuilt, good condition.
£3,500–4,000 *S*

TRIUMPH *(British)*

In 1902 Triumph began fitting Minerva, Fafnir and JAP engines to their bicycle frames to produce their first motorcycles. It was not until 1905 that they designed their own engine, a 300cc side valve, followed shortly by a 450cc and 475cc version. Sales rose quickly from 500 in 1906 to 3,000 in 1909. Several new models were added to the range from 1910 to 1920. The most successful of these models being the 550cc sv model H of which 30,000 were supplied to the British Army. During the 1920s Triumph produced the cheapest ever 500cc motorcycle in the world, the Model P which sold for £43. So successful was this bike that production levels rose to 1,000 per week.

In the early 1920s Triumph also entered into car manufacture, which proved not to be the wisest of moves. By the mid-20s the expensive car programme coupled with a slump in sales dragged the motorcycle division into jeopardy. In 1936 Triumph was sold to Jack Sangster, who immediately set out to redesign some of the older models. By the end of 1940, Triumph was successfully exporting bikes to the US, including the 650cc Thunderbird, 350cc and 500cc twins, 150cc Terrier and the 200cc Tiger Cub.

Despite these successes Triumph was sold to BSA in 1951. A series of problems developed which eventually led to BSA going bankrupt in 1973. Dennis Poore's Norton Villers group attempted to rescue Triumph with government aid, but the company finally foundered in 1983. John Bloor purchased all interests in Triumph and is now in full production with 3 and 4 cylinder water-cooled models.

1912 Triumph 490cc, single cylinder side valve 4 stroke engine, single speed belt driven, pedal assistance and starting, fitted leather tool boxes, very good condition, with original buff type log book.
Est. £4,000–5,000 *S*

1921 Triumph 498cc Solo.
£2,700–3,000 *LW*

1921 Triumph 498cc Solo.
£4,500–4,800 *LW*

1921 Triumph Model H.
£5,000–5,500 *AtMC*

1922 Triumph 'Baby' 225cc, 2 speed gearbox operated by a lever on the handlebars, restored to concours condition.
£4,700–5,200 *S*

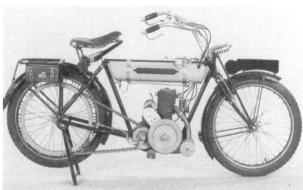

1923 Triumph 'Baby', 2 speed belt driven 2 stroke, fitted with a pair of leather fronted lockable tool boxes.
£2,900–3,300 *S*

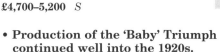

- Production of the 'Baby' Triumph continued well into the 1920s.
- Introduced in 1954 to meet demands from the north American market, the Tiger 110 was essentially a higher performance variant of the Thunderbird 650.
- Although the Tiger Cub engine shared much in design with the BSA C15, it retained the characteristic Triumph style.

1930 Triumph WL 350cc, single cylinder side valve 'sloper' engine, 3 speed gearbox, girder forks, rigid frame at rear, complete rebuild, good condition, old style log book.
Est. £3,200–3,500 *S*

c1924 Triumph Ricardo 4 valve.
£6,500–7,000 *AtMC*

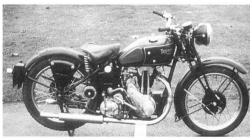

1934 Triumph 250cc Twin Port, good condition.
£1,800–2,100 *S*

Long before Edward Turner joined Triumph at Coventry, Val Page was designing classic machines for them (including a vertical twin). This little 250cc machine is a Val Page design with sporting twin port engine.

1936 Triumph L2/1 OHV Single Cylinder Sports 249cc, rebuilt 1975, needs slight restoration.
£1,800–2,200 *PS*

1937 Triumph Cinder 350cc, finished to Tiger specification black and silver with grey striping, chromium plated tank, high level exhaust system, good condition, buff log book.
£2,400–3,000 *S*

1938 Triumph Speed Twin 650cc, original girder forks and rear rigid frame, unrestored.
£1,500–1,800 *MR*

1938 Triumph 2H 250cc, overhead valve.
£2,900–3,600 *AT*

1939 Triumph Tiger 100 500cc, V-twin engine,
painted steel grey/blue, excellent condition.
£4,800–5,100 *S*

1939 Triumph 3SW 350cc Side Valve.
£1,400–1,800 *MVT*

1946 Triumph 5T Speed Twin 500cc, to
original specification, repainted maroon.
Est. £2,700–3,000 *S*

*This machine was purchased from a collector in
Delhi who owns the largest number of classic
motorcycles in India.*

1948 Triumph Speed Twin,
concours condition.
£5,500–6,000 *AtMC*

1948 Triumph 3T 350cc,
good original condition.
£1,600–1,900 *MR*

**1949 Triumph 3T 348cc Air Cooled Twin
Cylinder Overhead Valve 4 Stroke,**
finished in black with white striping,
chromium plated petrol tank, Triumph
nacelle and tank top parcel grid,
comprehensively overhauled.
£2,400–2,800 *S*

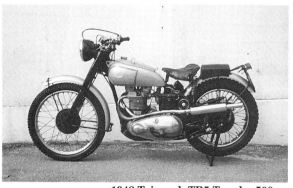

c1948 Triumph TR5 Trophy 500cc.
£2,300–2,600 *MR*

1951 Triumph Thunderbird 650cc.
£2,500–3,500   *WCM*

1952 Triumph Tiger 100 500cc, comprehensive restoration, CP100 kit, concours standard.
Est. £5,500–6,500   *S*

In its standard form the Tiger 100 offered exceptional performance, however, Edward Turner and Meriden perceived a market for a race equipped variant to compete in Clubman's and production racing. The kit was offered in two forms, the CP200 with 8.5:1 pistons and the CP100 with 8.25:1 piston. Other components included E3134 cams, Amal type 76 carburettors with a single remote float chamber and an oil tank of increased capacity. The result was an 8bhp increase over the standard 32bhp.

1952 Triumph Trophy Lookalike, all alloy Trophy engine, TRW frame, restored.
£2,750–3,000   *CBr*

1951 Triumph 6T Thunderbird 650cc, OHV twin with 'sprung hub' rear suspension.
£3,800–4,250   *AT*

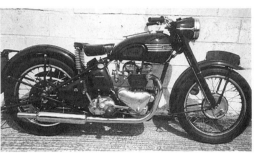

1953 Triumph Tiger 100, all alloy engine, sprung hub.
£3,000–3,500   *CBr*

1954 Triumph T110.
£2,800–4,200   *WCM*

1954 Triumph Tiger 110 650cc, finished in silver, blue and black colours, pivoted fork rear suspension, first class condition throughout.
£3,000–3,500 *S*

c1955 Triumph Trophy 500cc.
£6,000–6,500 *AtMC*

1955 Triumph T110 650cc.
£2,000–2,400 *PM*

c1955 Triumph Terrier Cub 149cc Racing Special, centrally mounted aluminum oil tank, single seat, full fairing, very good condition throughout.
£550–800 *S*

This machine was built and raced by Ron Purslow, before being passed to Leon Cooper, who also achieved considerable success.

1955 Triumph T100.
£3,250–3,600 *WCM*

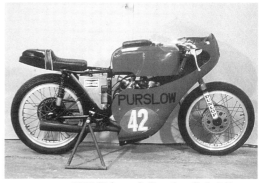

1956 Triumph 500cc, 5T engine, parts not strictly original, rebuilt.
Est. £1,700–1,900 *S*

1956 Triumph T110.
£4,700–5,000 *AtMC*

1957 Triumph T100 500cc Racer, fitted with twin Amal carburettors, finished in red with alloy rims, converted for road racing in vintage events.
Est. £1,500–2,000 *S*

1958 Triumph Tiger Cub 200cc T20, finished in silver and black, good cosmetic condition, mechanical condition unknown.
£470–800 *S*

1958 Triumph 21 'Bathtub' Model 350cc.
£1,500–1,800 *CBr*

1958 Tiger Cub T20 200cc, finished in red and silver, no known modifications from catalogue specification.
£500–800 *S*

1961 Triumph Cub T20 Roadster.
£750–850 *CBr*

1959 Triumph T120 Bonneville Pre-Unit 650cc Sports Twin, engine has higher lift sports camshafts, alloy splayed cylinder head, 2 monobloc carburettors minus float chambers fed by remote float chamber centrally mounted between, petrol tank, mudguards, oil tank and battery box finished in tangerine and pearl grey, restored.
£8,000–10,000 *HC*

1958 Triumph T120 Bonneville.
£5,500–6,500 *WCM*

1959 Triumph Tiger 110 650cc, rebuilt to a good standard, reconditioned magneto, dynamo and carburettor, the timing cover oil feed to crankshaft seal has been uprated, new chains and clutch replaced, finished in black and white.
£2,100–2,400 *S*

Newly introduced for 1954, the Tiger 110 had very few peers in the performance league.

1959 Triumph Trophy 650cc, high level exhaust, good mechanical condition, finished in white and red.
£5,600–6,000 *S*

1959 Triumph T20 Tiger Cub 200cc, high level exhaust system, red over grey petrol tank, grey mudguards and black frame, good condition throughout.
£900–1,200 *S*

1960 Triumph Thunderbird 650cc.
£2,200–3,000 *WCM*

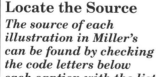

1960 Triumph T110 650cc.
£2,500–2,800 *PM*

1960 Triumph 3TA 350cc, finished in metallic blue.
£1,300–1,600 *HOLL*

Locate the Source
The source of each illustration in Miller's can be found by checking the code letters below each caption with the list of contributors.

1960 Triumph TR6R 650cc, restored.
£6,000–7,000 *WCM*

c1961 Triumph Tiger Cub 250cc, modified for use in trials, round cylinder head, with spare square head, good condition.
£700–900 *S*

1960 Triumph T120 Bonneville.
£4,500–6,000 *WCM*

1960 Triumph 5TA 490cc Speed Twin, fitted with a chrome headlight and sports mudguards, totally restored, very good condition throughout.
£1,700–2,000 *S*

1961 Triumph T120R Bonneville.
£4,500–6,500 *WCM*

1961 Triumph Thunderbird 'Bathtub' Model 650cc.
£3,750–4,100 *AT*

1961 Triumph T120 Bonneville 650cc, pre-unit engine, original except front brake.
£5,000–6,000 *BCB*

1961 Triumph Tiger 100 500cc,
excellent condition.
£2,700–3,000 *MR*

1961 Triumph Solo 350cc, several non-standard
parts fitted, largely complete but in need of
restoration.
£400–800 *S*

1961 Triumph TR6R, fully restored.
£6,300–6,600 *WCM*

1961 Triumph TR6R Trophy 650cc.
£4,500–6,000 *WCM*

> **Miller's is a price GUIDE
> not a price LIST**

1961 Triumph T120 Bonneville.
£6,000–7,000 *WCM*

**1962 Triumph Tiger Cub
199cc,** original.
£600–1,000 *PS*

1962 Triumph TR6SS 650cc.
£5,000–6,000 *WCM*
One of 1,304 produced in 1962.

1963 Triumph Cub Trials,
said to be ex-works.
£1,400–1,600 *CBr*

1963 Triumph Tiger Cub 200cc,
good condition.
£600–1,000 *PS*

1964 Triumph T120 Bonneville 650cc, high
compression engine, twin carburettors and
sporting styling.
£3,000–4,000 *RJES*

*This motorcyle gained its name from American,
Johnny Allen's, World Land Speed Record effort
in 1955 at the Bonneville Salt Flats in Utah,
producing 46bhp when introduced in the 1958
season. 1963 saw the end of the pre-unit range.*

1965 Triumph Tiger 90 350cc.
£1,500–1,900 *PM*

1965 Triumph T90 350cc.
£1,200–1,500 *PM*

1965 Triumph Sports Cub 200cc.
£1,600–2,000 *AtMC*

1966 Triumph Tiger 90 350cc.
£1,400–1,800 *PM*

1967 Triumph T90 350cc.
£1,300–1,500 *PM*

1966 Triumph T100 500cc, Daytona head
with twin carburettors, petrol tank finished in
green and white, white mudguards, black
frame, good condition.
£2,900–3,200 *S*

1967 Triumph Tiger 90 350cc, fully restored, good running order.
£1,400–1,800 *MR*

1967 Triumph Tiger Cub 200cc.
£800–1,200 *WCM*

This is one of the Bantam Cub Models using the BSA Bantam frame.

1967 Triumph T120 Bonneville.
£2,800–3,500 *WCM*

1968 Triumph Trophy 250cc.
£1,800–2,000 *AtMC*

1969 Triumph TR6 Trophy 650cc,
single carburettor, restored.
£2,700–3,000 *BCB*

c1968 Triumph T120C Bonneville 650cc American Market Model, 11:1 compression ratio, small tank, no lights, special cam, finished in burgundy and white, very good condition throughout.
£2,500–2,800 *S*

This machine is one of a series specially built for American flat track and TT racing under AMA rules.

1971 Triumph TR5C 500cc.
£2,000–2,300 *PM*

1970 Triumph T120R Bonneville,
unit construction, twin wind-tone horns fitted under the front of the petrol tank, 9 stud modified cylinder head carries two Amal concentric carburettors and twin pancake air filters, twin leading shoe front brake, finished in Astral red and silver, very good restored condition.
£4,000–4,500 *HC*

This was a very popular year as by 1970, after 11 years of the Bonneville run, many modifications had taken place.

1969 Triumph T100 490cc.
£1,200–1,500 *PS*

• Triumph's Trophy models underwent a significant change during the late 50s and early 60s moving away from their off road origins towards road use.
• Triumph's illustrious Bonneville proved to be not only an accomplished 'road burner', but with the aid of selective tuning and development, excellent in virtually all branches of motorcycle sport.

1972 Triumph TR6 649cc Tiger, vertical twin, air cooled, overhead valve, 4 stroke, 4 speed gearbox, chain final drive, telescopic front forks, pivoted fork Girling rear suspension, conical hubs, TLS front brake, restored.
£3,000–3,500 *OxM*

1972 Triumph T100R Daytona Unit Construction Twin 490cc, completely rebuilt in 1984, good running order.
£1,600–2,000 *PS*

Miller's is a price GUIDE
not a price LIST

1973 Triumph T120 650cc, big twin engine, telescopic forks, swinging arm rear suspension.
£1,000–1,300 *S*

1973 Triumph T140 Bonneville 750cc, clip-on handlebars, rear set footrests, Thruxton exhaust pipes and silencers, in excellent condition.
£2,200–2,500 *S*

c1974 Triumph Trident T150 750cc.
£3,000–3,500 *AtMC*

1974 Triumph Trident 750cc, originally an export model, totally rebuilt, excellent condition.
£4,500–5,000 *CRMC*

1976 Triumph T140 Bonneville 750cc,
UK specification tank, finished in blue and white.
£2,300–2,700 *S*

1974 Triumph Adventurer 500cc.
£2,500–3,000 *AtMC*

1976 Triumph T160 Trident 750cc,
3 cylinders, original except for alloy wheel rims.
£2,500–3,500 *BCB*

1979 Triumph Bonneville T140 750cc,
finished in smoked red and black, excellent condition.
Est. £2,800–3,500 *S*

This example of Triumph's illustrious Bonneville features the electric start that was introduced on the model in 1979, and is to domestic specification.

VELOCETTE *(British)*

Velocette was established in 1904 but it was not until 1913 that the company established itself with the production of a 206cc 2 stroke. The 2 stroke series, which eventually included a 220cc and 250cc, performed well in trials, speed hill climbs and the TT. Sporting successes throughout the 1920s and 30s did much to publicise Velocette motorcycles and hence the sales of road-going bikes increased. Models such as the KTS and KSS overhead camshaft were popular and sold until 1947. The rod high camshaft series did well with the 250cc MOV and 350cc MAC of 1933 and the 500cc MSS of 1935.

During the 1950s and 60s Velocette continued to develop outstanding racing bikes such as the Viper and Venom which they then called the Clubman racing versions. Despite what appeared to be a going concern the company did make several bad decisions and Velocette went into liquidation in 1968.

1934 Velocette MAC 350cc.
£2,500–3,000 *AtMC*

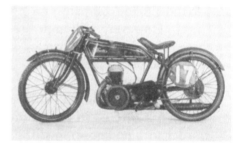

1924 Velocette HSS 249cc Ex-Works Racer, 2 stroke, old style log book.
£4,500–4,800 *S*

This is an historic racing machine with excellent provenance, a road racing works machine believed to be the only survivor of six made.

1938 Velocette KSS, overhead cam sportster, in traditional black and gold livery, good condition.
Est. £4,700–5,000 *S*

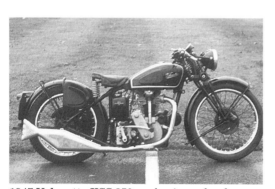

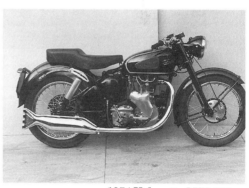

1954 Velocette MSS 500cc.
£3,000–3,300 *VER*

1947 Velocette KSS 350cc, classic overhead camshaft single cylinder engine, 4 speed gearbox, finished in black paintwork, excellent condition, old style log book.
£3,200–3,500 *S*

1956 Velocette Viper 350cc Scrambler, trials tyres and speedo, black paintwork and gold lettering, totally rebuilt and restored.
£4,300–4,600 *S*

Believed to be one of only 25 built.

c1960 Velocette Viper 350cc.
£2,500–3,000 AtMC

1958 Velocette Valiant 200cc, overhead valve horizontally opposed air cooled twin cylinder, black paintwork and chrome, good condition mechanically.
£1,000–1,300 S

YAMAHA (Japanese)

The logo of the three tuning forks should make the origin of Yamaha motorcycles obvious to most, but if there had not been excess room in the foundry where the company cast their piano frames this story may never have needed to be told. The first Yamaha motorcycle, built in 1954, was a copy of a 125cc DKW RT 125 2 stroke. In 1959 they produced a tubular framed YDS1, a 250cc twin with 5 speed gearbox, that was used by the company for the next 20 years.

During the 1960s Yamaha achieved total domination of the 250cc and 350cc classes and in the Grand Prix series they created the most effective 2 strokes seen at that time and many claim they alone were responsible for the development of the modern racing 2 stroke still being used today. Directly related to their sports successes was the marketing success of their road-going bikes. Between 1960 and 70 they were the market leader of 2 stroke road machines from 50cc to 350cc. When anti-pollution laws were enforced in the US they quickly developed a 4 stroke engine which soon grew into a full series of single cylinder engines, twins, 3s and 4s.

1969 Yamaha TZA 250cc Racer, 2 stroke twin cylinder engine, good condition, throughout.
Est. £2,750–3,000 S

1967 Yamaha YDS 5E 246cc, twin cylinder air cooled 2 stroke, excellent condition both mechanically and cosmetically, red painted petrol tank and sidepanels, chrome and polished alloy finish.
£2,600–3,000 S

c1969 Yamaha TR2 350cc Solo Racer, air cooled twin cylinder 2 stroke, finished in traditional racing colours of red and white, restored to original specification.
£3,600–4,000 S

1976 Yamaha XT500 OHC 497cc, single cylinder Enduro/Trail, original condition apart from front mudguard.
£700–900 PS

ZENITH *(British)*

1916 Zenith Gradua 770cc, JAP V-twin engine, original specification apart from exhaust pipes, and thrust ball race on the engine pulley, finished in black, good condition throughout.
£7,100–7,500 *S*

1922 Zenith 980cc, side valve JAP V-twin and belt drive, finished in black and green to a high standard.
Est. £9,000–9,500 *S*

SPECIALS

1932 BSA Sports Twin 1020cc 3 Wheeler,
Est. £10,000–11,000
and a 1945 BSA M20.
£7,000–8,000 *EM*

1969 BSA B50 Special 499cc, grafted on 5 speed gearbox, one-off frame, disc front brake, alloy petrol and oil tanks.
£2,500–2,700 *PC*

1986 Ducati-Metisse Café racer, specially commissioned Rickman Metisse chassis, Ducati 860GT V-twin engine, Marzocchi suspension.
£2,500–3,000 *PC*

1984 Ducati-Harris Special, Harris frame, Ducati 900SS bevel V-twin engine.
£4,000–4,500 *PC*

One of a small batch built by Sports Racing of Macclesfield, Cheshire.

1938 James Handy Van 8 cwt, air cooled V-twin engine, 1096cc, electric starter and unique hand start next to driver's door, full history.
£4,500–6,000 *AT*

Mini Honda 70cc Racing Special, bored
out to 70cc, 4 stroke 50cc single engine,
3 speed gearbox, tubular frame with mono
shock rear suspension, telescopic forks,
finished in Honda racing colours, good
condition throughout, 18in (46cm) high.
£550–600 *S*

1938 Morgan 1000cc OHV.
£14,000–15,000 *VER*

**1967 Matchless-Norton Special
497cc,** overhead valve Matchless
engine, AMC gearbox, Norton
Dominator frame and front brake,
Manx rear brake, tank and seat.
£2,500–3,000 *PC*

1954 Norton International 490cc Solo,
overhead camshaft, air-cooled, 4 stroke vertical
single engine, 4 speed gearbox, Norton
Featherbed wideline frame, chain final drive,
John Tickle TLS front brake, telescopic
Roadholder front forks, pivoted fork rear
suspension, hand built.
£5,500–6,000 *OxM*

**c1960 Norton Dominator 850cc 'Special'
Hybrid Café Racer,** Commando Interstate
engine, Dominator Featherbed frame/tank,
Norton Manx wheels.
£7,000–8,000 *HM*

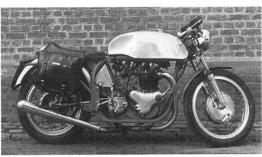

**c1960 Norton Dominator 650cc Solo Café
Racer,** vertical twin cylinder, air-cooled, overhead
valve, 4 stroke, 4 speed AMC gearbox, chain final
drive, Norton telescopic Roadholder forks, pivoted
fork rear suspension, Norton Featherbed slimline
frame, hand-built.
£1,800–2,000 *OxM*

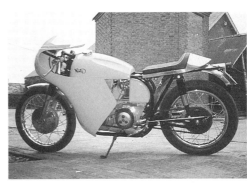

c1960 Norton Jawa 500cc Solo Café Racer,
vertical single air-cooled, double overhead
camshaft, 4 valve, 4 stroke, 4 speed AMC
gearbox, chain final drive, Norton telescopic
Roadholder forks, pivoted fork rear suspension,
Norton Featherbed wideline frame, Jawa
competition engine, hand-built.
£2,000–2,500 *OxM*

1964 Norton 650cc SS Solo, overhead valve, air-cooled, 4 stroke vertical twin Dunstallized engine, Norton Featherbed slimline frame, chain final drive, telescopic Norton Roadholder forks, pivoted fork rear suspension, hand-built.
£3,500–4,000 *OxM*

c1965 Petty Manx 350cc Racer, Manx overhead camshaft engine, built by Ray Petty using his own frame, excellent condition, fully rebuilt, rare with good provenance.
Est. £12,000–12,500 *S*

1977 Triumph T140V Bonneville Special, overhead valve, air-cooled, 4 stroke vertical twin engine, 5 speed gearbox, chain final drive, telescopic front forks, pivoted fork rear suspension, hydraulic brakes, mild custom.
£1,600–1,800 *OxM*

c1960 Norton Matchless 500cc Solo Café Racer, Matchless G80CS engine, vertical single, air-cooled, overhead valve, 4 stroke, 4 speed AMC gearbox, chain final drive, Norton telescopic Roadholder forks, pivoted fork rear suspension, 4LS front brake, Norton Featherbed wideline frame, unfinished, hand-built.
£2,500–2,800 *OxM*

1955 NSU Max Special 247cc, overhead camshaft, Max engine converted to Sportmax specification, Sportmax alloy replica tank, Amal carburettor, alloy wheel rims.
£2,000–2,200 *PC*
This bike is CRMC registered.

1967 Rickman-Aermacchi 344cc racer, overhead valve, nickel plated frame, Lockheed disc front brake, Dell'Orto carburettor, 5 speed gearbox.
£7,700–8,000 *PC*

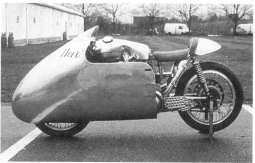

c1950 Vincent 'Nero' 998cc Racer, excellent running order.
£56,000+ *S*

SIDECARS

1930 Brough-Superior SS80 998cc Combination, 85.7 x 85mm bore and stroke V-twin, stripped paintwork, 'cruiser' sidecar, Bentley and Draper sprung rear end, bevel driven magneto.
£6,500–6,800 *S*

1958 Ariel Square Four Combination, finished in silver over black, with Watsonian Oxford double adult sidecar, good condition.
£4,700–5,000 *S*

1916 BSA 4¼hp 575cc Combination, side valve single cylinder 4 stroke, finished in BSA's traditional green livery, fitted with full carbide lighting set, single seat sidecar, canvas hood, in good condition throughout.
£4,700–5,000 *S*

1922 BSA Model K2 550cc Combination, original condition, with panniers and full acetylene lighting set, original buff log book.
Est. £3,500–4,500 *S*

1926 BSA 'K' Series 557cc Combination, original and unrestored.
£3,500–4,000 *Bro*

c1958 BSA Gold Star 499cc 'Works Supported' Trials Combination, Goldie engine with Amal 389 Monobloc, Earles leading link front forks, special combined frame and sidecar chassis with all-round suspension, good condition throughout.
Est. £5,000–7,000 *S*

This well documented machine was built by Frank Darrieulat, the 1958 ACU Trials Drivers Star Holder, between 1958–59, and was campaigned by him during the 1959 season. Its history and pedigree are well documented and it has been featured in Classic Motorcycle *and the* Book of BSA History.

c1967 Ex-WD BSA B40 Single Cylinder Trials Outfit, 343cc, Bultaco front fork and wheel, alloy wheel rims, trials tyres, spoked alloy wheel on sidecar, reasonable condition.
£700–900 *PS*

1964 Greeves 25DD Essex and Watsonian YSI Single Seat Sidecar, finished in blue, fitted with fork spats, restored, excellent condition.
£3,500–4,000 *S*

Bert Greeves' Thundersley based firm's products displayed a certain independence in their design which set them apart from their other Villiers powered machines.

c1934 Norton Model 20 490cc Combination, low 'pie crust' tank, pillion seat and full lighting set, period 'launch' sidecar with boat decking on the upper surfaces and luggage rail, finished in classic Norton livery of black and silver with red lining, sidecar in black, original condition.
£3,700–4,000 *S*

1958 BMW R50/Steib Combination, paintwork in black, original tool kit, instruction manual and cockpit cover, very good condition throughout.
Est. **£4,500–6,000** *LF*

BMW caused something of a sensation when they introduced the R50 (500cc) and R69 (600cc) at the Brussels Salon in January, 1955. These machines were the best that BMW had yet offered. The Earles type front forks and full swinging arm rear suspension closely resembled the factory racers, whilst the rear frame, although similar to the old plunger design, had been totally revised to produce an extremely rigid frame for the benefit of sidecar users.

Did you know?
MILLER'S Classic Motorcycles Price Guide *builds up year-by-year to form the most comprehensive photo library system available.*

1923 New Imperial 986cc Combination, 8hp V-twin engine, Burman 3 speed gearbox, finished in correct New Imperial livery of Brunswick green, black and gold, very good condition throughout.
£9,500–10,000 *S*

Sidecar coachwork by Mills & Fulford and features loop frame introduced on New Imperial machines in November 1922.

MOPEDS

1914 Autoped, registered 1922, engine above front wheel, lacks saddle, some renovation.
£2,600–2,900 *S*

c1940 Cyc-Auto 98cc Pedal Assisted, original, missing fuel lines to Amal carburettor and inlet manifold to the cylinder, Bates saddle and rear luggage carrier.
£250–350 *S*

Produced from 1934–56, Scott's Cyc-Auto moped was powered by a 98cc 2 stroke engine mounted in a substantial bicycle frame with pressed steel front forks and coil spring front suspension.

1965 Raleigh Runabout Moped, original saddle and tool bag, finished in original cream and dark green livery.
Est. £100–150 *S*

1955 NSU Quickly Moped, leading link front forks and rigid spine frame, optional windscreen and legshields.
£350–500 *S*

These machines were largely responsible for the demise of the 'clip-on' engine and cyclemotors, the German NSU Quickly proving immensely popular with well over one million examples being manufactured between 1953 and 1962.

1974 Italjet Pack 2 49cc, designed to be stowed and carried, very light, good condition.
£200–300 *PS*

SCOOTERS

1948 Corgi 98cc, original, unrestored condition, complete.
£700–800 *S*

Developed from the wartime 'Welbike', which spent its military career being thrown out of aeroplanes in the company of the Parachute Regiment, the Brockhouse Corgi featured a 98cc engine and folding handlebars, which with its diminutive size and fuel consumption endeared it to many in the austere post-war years.

c1950 Corgi 98cc, Excelsior MkI engine, folding handlebars and retracting seat.
£250–350 *S*

1954 MV Agusta 124cc, with pillion seat, finished in light blue, professionally restored to high standard, excellent condition.
Est. £2,150–2,200 *S*

It is perhaps not generally known in the UK that the MV Agusta company built motor scooters in Italy, and they were never common here. This scooter is a Second Series type.

c1948 Corgi 98cc Folding Motor Scooter, fair condition.
£550–600 *S*

c1958 Terrot, 125cc.
£50–200 *RSk*

1951 MV Agusta 124cc, with single seat, original maroon paintwork, complete, good condition, unrestored.
Est. £1,150–1,250 *S*

This example of MV's First Series scooter is extremely rare, and differs in considerable detail to the Second Series machine, having a duplex frame at rear. A rare and early machine.

1957 Zündapp Bella 200cc,
working speedo, runs well.
£150–200 *RSk*

1957 TWN Contessa 200cc, air-cooled, split single, 2 stroke with pivoted form front and rear suspension, unit engine and gearbox, 4 speed gearbox, footchange, electric starter.
Est. £800–1,000 *RJES*

c1958 Lambretta LD 150cc, running, needs restoration.
£150–200 *RSk*

1959 Vespa 150.
£100–150 *RSk*

1959 Lambretta LI 150cc Series I.
£150–200 *RSk*

c1960 NSU Prima III.
£75–100 *RSk*

1959 Lambretta LI 150cc Series I, running, needs restoration.
£250–300 *RSk*

RESTORATION PROJECTS

1914 Matchless Model 900 903cc V-Twin,
engine rebuilt, complete but dismantled.
£2,600–3,000 *S*

1913 Matchless 976cc Combination, JAP
rebuilt engine, dismantled, restored and believed
to be complete, single seat sidecar unrestored,
original logbook.
£4,000–4,500 *S*

1927 Scott Super Squirrel 598cc, mechanically
sound, in need of restoration.
£1,400–1,600 *S*

**1951 Vincent Comet OHV Single
Cylinder 499cc,** in need of restoration.
£2,400–2,800 *PS*

1959 AJS 650cc, overhead valve twin
cylinder engine, complete, original
condition, old style logbook.
Est. £550–600 *S*

**c1971 BSA A70 Lightning 751cc Grass
Track Racer,** A70 vertical twin overhead
valve engine and 4 speed gearbox, one of only
200 built for US, complete.
Est. £3,000–4,000 *S*

1972 Triumph TR6 650cc Tiger Solo,
vertical twin, 71 x 82mm bore and stroke,
air-cooled, overhead valve 4 stroke, 4 speed
gearbox, chain final drive, telescopic front
forks, pivoted fork Girling rear suspension,
conical hubs, TLS front brake, first of
Meriden's 'oil in frame' model twin.
£350–450 *OxM*

MOTORCYCLE MEMORABILIA

A collection of Douglas Sales Catalogues and Leaflets, mostly 1930s, and a Lambretta leaflet.
£170–200 *S*

The Light Car & Cyclecar Journal, 23rd April, 1917, illustrated, original price 1d.
£30–40 *MCh*

Further Motorcycle Reminiscences, published 1928, 7½ x 5in (19 x 12.5cm).
£25–30 *PMB*

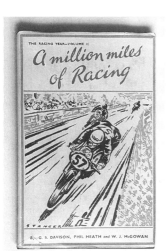

A Million Miles of Racing, G. S. Davison, Phil Heath and W. J. McGowan, mint condition, 7 x 5in (17.5 x 12.5cm).
£20–25 *PMB*

A Triumph Motorcycle Brochure, 1932, 10 x 7½in (25 x 19cm).
£20–25 *PMB*

A Michelin Colour Lithograph Poster, after F. Fabriano, on linen, published by Chaiz, 1916, 47 x 30in (119 x 76cm).
£370–400 *ONS*

A Griffon Cycles, Motos, Tricars Colour Lithograph Poster, after Thor, published by G. Elleaume, Paris, 31½ x 47in (80 x 118cm).
Est. £400–600 *ONS*

A 1959 Excelsior Brochure, 9½ x 5½in (24 x 14cm).
£5–8 *PMB*

A 1953 Matchless Brochure, 6 x 8in (15 x 20cm).
£10–15 *PMB*

New-Hudson Motorcycles,
chromolithograph, full colour,
c1925, 30 x 20in (76 x 50.5cm).
Est. £350–450 *BKS*

Marcello Nizzoli, 1927
Motosacoche, original poster,
50½ x 35¾in (128 x 91cm).
£470–520 *S*

New-Hudson Motorcycles,
Your Final Choice,
chromolithograph, c1925,
30 x 20in (76 x 50.5cm).
Est. £200–300 *BKS*

**A Triumph Works Team Photograph, Senior
TT Race, 1921,** on a display mount marked with
details of the riders, 10 x 12in (25 x 30.5cm), framed
and glazed.
£330–350 *S*

René Vincent (1879–1936),
original poster design,
watercolour and gouache,
Ce Que J'ai Vu Par Bibendum,
13½ x 10⅛in (35 x 27cm) framed.
£1,400–1,600 *S*

**A National Benzole Advertising
Calendar,** embossed cardboard
sign with Mercury symbol and card
date/month display, 1930s, 15⅛in
(38cm) high.
£280–300 *S*

**A Francis-Barnett
Illuminated Sign,**
10¾ x 14in (27 x 36cm).
£110–130 *S*

**A Portable Michelin
Bibendum Tyre
Compressor,** French, No.
27795 DB, 110 volts, with
2 pin plug and inflation
gauges, 11½in (29cm) long.
£420–450 *S*

A Colour Lithograph Poster,
after Geo. Ham, Dunlop Pneus
Moto, 1930, on linen,
47 x 32in (119 x 81cm).
Est. 200–300 *ONS*

**A Quantity of Motorcycle
Advertising Posters,** reprints,
together with a pen and ink
drawing dated 23. Aug. 1934,
framed and glazed, a collection of
reference cards of motorcycle line
drawings, assorted calendars and
other ephemera.
£40–60 *S*

Rod Organ, Mountain Mile,
oil on canvas, signed and dated
1988, depicting Joey Dunlop at the
1985 F1 TT on a 750cc RVF Honda,
19¾ x 29½in (50 x 75cm).
£420–450 *S*

Phil May, Grand Prix
Internationale Autos-
Motorrader, Berne, 1966,
signed print from an original
poster design, 16 x 11in
(41 x 28cm), mounted,
framed and glazed.
Est. £60–100 *S*

**A Poster for a Circuit de
Saint-Cloud,** 9th June, 1946.
Est. £300–400 *ONS*

**A Collection of Motorcycling
photographs,** depicting races,
events, machines including
Excelsior Junior and riders,
some reprints.
£50–70 *S*

**A Collection of Motorcycling
photographs,** depicting races
including 1913 Grand Prix de
France de Motos Le Mans, other
events, machines and riders,
some reprints.
£150–200 *S*

**A Collection of Isle of Man TT
Photographs,** black and white,
some reprints.
£140–160 *S*

**A Collection of Photographs
of Motorcyclists and
Personalities,** including
Geoff Duke, Barry Sheene,
Mike Hailwood, A. J. Bell,
George Dance, Kenny Roberts,
H. L. Daniel and others,
some reprints.
£130–150 *S*

**A Collection of Motorcycling
Photographs,** depicting races
including 1921 Grand Prix de
France, other events, machines
and riders, some reprints.
£130–150 *S*

**Ten Original Motorcycle
Illustrations,** by Harold
Connolly, watercolour, c1962,
including a colour design
depicting Douglas 1913, the
remainder monochrome
including Brooklands Memory
1928, all signed, many with
descriptive captions.
Est. £400–500 *S*

A selection of four Petrol Pump Globes.
£80–250 each   *S*

A Pair of Motorcycle Trophies,
each a silver plated statuette of a
motorcycle and rider, mounted on a
wooden block, applied with silver
plated plaque, one engraved 'To a
master', the other 'From a student
24.10.36', 4in (10cm) high.
£240–260   *S*

**A Cromwell Protector
Fibre Crash Helmet,** size 7,
with Matchless transfer.
£75–90   *ONS*

Michelin Man,
'Monsieur Bibendum'.
£120–140   *MCh*

A Silver Plated Salver,
British Motorcycle Racing
Club, Brooklands, awarded to
Eric Fernihough, Fastest Lap,
1935, 123.58mph (Brough-
Superior Motorcycle).
£250–350   *MCh*

Rod Organ, signed, dated '90',
oil on canvas, depicting Stanley
Woods on the works Mk 8 KTT
Velocette, riding through St.
Ninians crossroads at speed
during the 1939 Junior TT,
19¾ x 29½in (50 x 75cm), signed
on back of canvas by Stanley
Woods, framed.
Est. £1,000-1,200   *S*

**A selection of Automobile
Associaton Badges,**
1907–30.
£50–250 each   *MCh*

**Ten Original Harold Connolly Watercolour
Motorcycle Illustrations,** c1962, including a colour
design depicting Zenith-Bradshaw 1923, the remainder
monochrome including American X 1921, all signed,
many with descriptive captions.
Est. £400–600   *S*

**A 1914 Copper Pressed Advertising
Calendar,** for Witt & Bird, Motorcycling and
Motoring Outfitters.
£120–140   *MCh*

**A 'Shell Shortens Every Road'
enamel sign,** 36 x 72in
(91.5 x 182.5cm).
£290–320 *S*

A Collection of Oil Tins.
£50–100 each *S*

**A Shell 'Fill up Here' Enamel
Sign,** some chips and rust,
48in (122cm) square.
£470–500 *S*

**A Scott 3 Cylinder 2 Stroke
Motorcycle Engine,** water-cooled
monobloc, c1941, rare, with
contemporary press reports.
£1,700–2,000 *S*

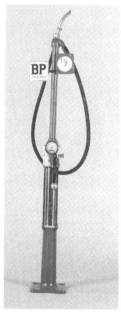

**A Hand-Operated
Avery–Hardoll
Petrol Pump,** model
CH1, patent 306358/28
with delivery dial,
lacking needle, painted
blue with BP price flag,
84in (213cm) high, with
hose and nozzle.
£500–550 *S*

**A Scott Sociable 578cc Engine
and Gearbox,** 76.2 x 63.3mm
bore and stroke, twin cylinder
unit mounted on a Scott Sociable
wheel, twin plug heads, hand
starter lever for engine, water
pump for cooling, twin plug
magneto, with frame and fittings.
Est. £800–900 *S*

**A Selection of Items belonging to
the late Sir Malcolm Campbell:**
A framed and glazed Dominion Tyre
advertisement, signed. **£120–150**
A silver clothes brush, with monogram.
£100–150
A personal lighter, with monogram,
boxed. **£150–220** *MCh*

A Dunlop Foot Pump, c1925, brass and
black enamelled steel.
£80–140 *MCh*

A Castrol Lubricant Funnel, 1950s, enamelled steel,
with a copper levels filling funnel by Joseph Lucas Ltd.,
Birmingham, 1920s.
£90–120 *MCh*

Three Original Motorcycle Advertising Posters, for Ariel Red Hunter, James Cadet 150, Colonel 225 and BSA 250.
£220–250 *S*

An H. J. Goodwin Hand Cranked Petrol Pump, red with polished brass, fitted with Shell price flag sticker, Goodyear hose, restored, with a modern 'Fat' Sealed Shell glass globe, 100in (254cm) high overall.
Est. £1,000–1,400 *S*

An Agents for Ariel advertising sign, transfer printed glass plate in metal hanging frame, 14in (35.5cm) wide.
£130–150 *S*

A Lodge Spark Plug Holder, with a set of six 18mm unused Lodge Spark plugs, c1920s.
£80–120 *MCh*

A 'Perfection' Oil Cabinet for Vacuum Mobiloil, corrugated drum, hinged lid, repainted green, 41½in (105cm) high, with pump and wooden dipstick.
£400–600 *S*

A Carmarthen Motor Cycle & Light Car Club Member's Badge, chrome plated and enamelled.
£60–80 *MCh*

An Alexandra's Spare Bulbs Carrier, brass, c1920s.
£60–80 *MCh*

A Retailer's Dunlop Tube & Tyre Repair Outfit Dispensing Case, with repair outfit tins.
£100–140 *MCh*

Ten Original Motorcycle Illustrations, by Harold Connolly, watercolour, c1962, including a colour design depicting Brough-Superior SS80, 1925, with monochrome 'The End' design to reverse, the remainder monochrome including Brough-Superior 'Golden Dream' 1928, all signed, many with descriptive captions.
Est. £400–600 *S*

GLOSSARY

We have attempted to define some of the terms that you will come across in this book. If there are any other terms or technicalities you would like explained or you feel should be included in future editions, please let us know.

ACU - Auto Cycle Union, who control a large part of British motorcycle sport.

Advanced ignition - Ignition timing set causing firing before the piston reaches centre top, variation is now automatic.

Air-cooling - Most motorcycles rely on air-cooling to the atmosphere.

Air intake - The carburettor port admitting air to mix with fuel from the float chamber.

AMCA - Amateur Motor Cycle Association, promoters of English off-road events.

APMC - The Association of Pioneer Motor Cyclists.

Auto Cycle Club - Formed in 1903 it was the original governing body of motorcycle sport, in 1907 became the Auto Cycle Union.

Automatic inlet valve - Activated by the engine suction. Forerunner of the mechanically operated valve.

Balloon tyres - Wide section, low pressure, soft running tyres, used on tourers for comfort.

Beaded-edge tyres - Encased rubber beads in channel on wheel rim.

Belt drive - A leather or fabric belt from engine or gearbox to rear wheel.

BHP - A measure of engine output, e.g. to lift 33,000lb one foot in a minute requires one horsepower.

BMCRC - British Motor Cycle Racing Club, formed in 1909.

BMF - British Motorcycle Federation.

Bore/stroke ratio - Cylinder diameter ratio to stroke.

Cam - Device for opening and closing a valve.

Camshaft - The mounting shaft for the cam, can be in low, high or overhead position.

Carburettor - Used to produce the air/fuel mixture.

Chain drive - Primary form of drive from engine to gearbox and secondary gearbox to rear wheel.

Combustion chamber - Area where the fuel/air mixture is compressed and fired, between piston and cylinder head.

Compression ratio - The fuel/air mixture compression degree.

Crankcase - The casing enclosing the crankshaft and its attachments.

Crankshaft - The shaft for converting the up-and-down piston motion into rotary.

Cylinder - Containing the piston and capped by the cylinder head, is the site of the explosion which provides power.

Cylinder head - In a vertical engine caps off the top end of the cylinder. In a 4 stroke engine carries the valves.

Damper - Used for slowing down movement in suspension system or as crankshaft balance.

Displacement - The engine capacity or amount of volume displaced by the movement of the piston from bottom dead centre to top dead centre.

Distributor - A gear driven contact sending high tension current to spark plugs.

DOHC - Double overhead camshaft.

Dry sump - Two oil pumps, one supplying oil to the bearings from a tank, the other to return it to the tank.

Earles forks - An unusual front fork design. A long leading link and rigid pivot through both links behind the wheel.

Featherbed - A Norton frame, designed by Rex and Crommie McCandless, Belfast, used for racing machines from 1950, road machines from 1953.

FIM - Federation Internationale Motorcycliste, controls motorcycle sport worldwide.

Flat head - A flat surfaced cylinder head.

Flat twin - An engine with 2 horizontally opposed cylinders, or 4 to make a Flat Four.

Float - A plastic or brass box which floats upon the fuel in a float chamber and operates the needle valve controlling the fuel.

Flywheel - Attached to the crankshaft this heavy wheel smooths intermittent firing impulses and helps slow running.

Friction drive - An early form of drive using discs in contact instead of chains and gears.

Gearbox - Cased trains of pinion wheels which can be moved to provide alternative ratios.

Gear ratios - Differential rates of speed between sets of pinions to provide higher or lower rotation of the rear wheel in relation to the engine.

GP - Grand Prix, an international race to a fixed formula.

High camshaft - Mounted high up on the engine to shorten the pushrods in an ohv formation.

IOE - Inlet over exhaust, a common arrangement with an overhead inlet and side exhaust.

Leaf spring - Metal blades clamped and bolted together, used in suspension many years ago.

Magneto - A high tension dynamo producing current for the ignition spark. Superseded by coil ignition.

Main bearings - Bearings in which the crankshaft runs.

Manifold - Collection of pipes supplying mixture or taking away fumes.

MCC - The Motor Cycling club which runs sporting events. Formed in 1902.

Moped - A light motorcycle of under 50cc with pedals attached.

OHC - Overhead camshaft, can be either single or double.

OHV - Overhead valve engine.

Overhead cam - An engine with overhead camshaft or camshafts operating its valves.

Overhead valve - A valve mounted in the cylinder head.

Pinking - A distinctive noise from an engine with over-advanced ignition or inferior fuel.

Piston - The component driven down the cylinder by expanding gases.

Post-vintage - A motorcycle made after December 31, 1930 and before January 1, 1945.

Pressure plate - The plate against which the clutch springs react to load the friction plates.

Pushrods - Operating rods for overhead valves, working from cams below the cylinder.

Rotary valve - A valve driven from the camshaft for inlet or exhaust and usually a disc or cylinder shape. For either 2 or 4 stroke engines.

SACU - Scottish Auto Cycle Union, which controls motorcyle sport in Scotland.

SAE - Society of Automotive Engineers. Used in a system of classifying engine oils such as SAE30, IOW/50 etc.

Shock absorber - A damper, used to control up-and-down movement of suspension or to cushion a drive train.

Swinging arm - Rear suspension by radius arms carrying the wheel and attached to the frame at the other end.

Torque - Twisting rotational force in a shaft, can be measured to show at what point an engine develops most torque.

INDEX TO ADVERTISERS

BIBLIOGRAPHY

Bacon, Roy; Matchless & AJS Restoration, Osprey, 1993.
Bacon, Roy; Norton Twin Restoration, Osprey, 1993.
Bacon, Roy; Triumph Twins & Triples, Osprey, 1990.
Birkitt, Malcolm; Harley-Davidson, Osprey, 1993.
Morley, Don; and Woollett, Mick; Classic Motorcycles, BMW, Osprey, 1992.
Morley, Don; Classic Motorcycles, Triumph, Osprey, 1991.
Stuart, Garry; and Carroll, John; Classic Motorcycles, Indian, Osprey, 1994.
Tragatsch, Erwin, ed; The New Illustrated Encyclopedia of Motorcycles, Grange Books, 1993.
Walker, Mick; Classic Motorcycles, Honda, Osprey, 1993.

Walker, Mick; Classic European Racing Motorcycles, Osprey, 1992.
Walker, Mick; Classic Italian Racing Motorcycles, Osprey, 1991.
Walker, Mick; Classic Japanese Racing Motorcycles, Osprey, 1991.
Walker, Mick; Classic Motorcycles, Ducati, Osprey, 1993.
Walker, Mick; Classic Motorcycles, Kawasaki, Osprey, 1993.
Walker, Mick; Classic Motorcycles, Suzuki, Osprey, 1993.
Walker, Mick; Classic Motorcycles, Yamaha, Osprey, 1993.
Wherrett, Duncan; Classic Motorcycles, Vincent, Osprey, 1994.
Woollett, Mick; Norton, Osprey, 1992.

DIRECTORY OF MOTORCYCLE CLUBS

If you wish to be included in next year's directory or if you have a change of address or telephone number, please could you inform us by April 30th 1995. Entries will be repeated in subsequent editions unless we are requested otherwise.

AJS & Matchless Owners Club,
25 Bevington Close,Patchway,
Bristol, Avon
AMC Owners Club, c/o Terry Corley,
12 Chilworth Gardens, Sutton, Surrey
Androd Classics, 70 Broadway,
Frome, Somerset
Tel: 01373 471087
Ariel Owners Club, c/o Mike Taylor,
Harrow House, Woolscott, Rugby,
Warwicks
Bantam Enthusiasts Club,
c/o Vic Salmon, 16 Oakhurst Close,
Walderslade, Chatham, Kent
Benelli Owners Club, c/o Rosie
Marston, 14 Rufford Close, Barton
Seagrave, Kettering, Northants
BMW Owners Club, c/o Mike Cox,
22 Combermere, Thornbury, Bristol
Bristol & District Sidecar Club,
158 Fairlyn Drive, Kingswood,
Bristol, Avon
Bristol Genesis Motorcycle Club,
Burrington, 1a Bampton Close,
Headley Park, Bristol
Tel: 0117 978 2584
Bristol Micro Car Club, 123 Queens
Road, Bishopsworth, Bristol
Tel: 0117 964 2901
British Two Stroke Owners Club,
c/o Mark Hathaway, 45 Moores Hill,
Olney, Bucks
British Motorcyclists Federation,
129 Seaforth Avenue, Motspur Park,
New Malden, Surrey
British Motor Bike Owners,
c/o Ray Peacock, Crown Inn,
Shelfanger, Diss, Norfolk
British Motorcycle Owners,
c/o Phil Coventry, 59 Mackenzie
Street, Bolton
Brough Superior Club,
c/o Piers Otley, 6 Canning Road,
Felpham, West Sussex
BSA Owners Club, c/o Rob Jones,
44 Froxfield Road, West Leigh,
Havant, Hants
CBX Riders Club, c/o Peter Broad, 57
Osborne Close, Basingstoke,
Hampshire
**Christian Motorcyclists
Association,** PO Box 113,
Wokingham, Berkshire
Classic Motor Cycle Racing Club,
c/o Simon Wilson, 6 Pendennis Road,
Freshbrook, Swindon, Wiltshire
Tel: 01793 610828
Cossack Owners Club,
c/o Dorothy Noble, 67 Charnock,
Skelmersdale, Lancs
DKW Rotary Owners Club,
c/o David Cameron, Dunbar,
Ingatestone Road, Highwood,
Chelmsford, Essex
Douglas Owners Club,
c/o Reg Holmes, 48 Standish Avenue,
Stoke Lodge, Patchway, Bristol, Avon
Ducati Owners Club, 131 Desmond
Drive, Old Catton, Norwich
Dunstall Owners Club,
c/o Barry Hutchinson, PO Box 51,
Prestwick, Manchester
Featherbed Specials Owners Club,
Maytham Farm, Maytham Road,
Rolvenden, Cranbrook, Kent
Francis Barnett Owners Club,
58 Knowle Road, Totterdown, Bristol
Gold Star Owners Club, c/o Brian
Shackleford, 88 Hykham Road, Lincoln
Goldwing Owners Club GB,
82 Farley Close, Little Stoke, Bristol

Greeves Owners Club,
c/o Dave McGregor, 4 Longshaw Close,
North Wingfield, Chesterfield,
Derbyshire
Greeves Riders Association,
40 Swallow Park, Thornbury, Avon
Tel: 01454 418037
Harley Davidson Owners Club,
1 St Johns Road, Clifton, Bristol
**Harley Davidson Riders Club of
Great Britain,** Membership
Secretary, PO Box 62, Newton Abbott,
Devon
Hesketh Owners Club,
c/o Peter White, 1 Northfield Road,
Soham, Cambs
Honda Owners Club,
c/o Dave Barton, 18a Embley Close,
Calmore, Southampton
Indian Motorcycle Club GB, Surrey
Mills, Chilworth, Guildford, Surrey
**International CBX Owners
Association,** 24 Pevensey Way,
Paddock Hill, Frimley,
Camberley, Surrey
Tel: 01252 836698
**International Laverda Owners
Club,** c/o Alan Cudipp, Orchard
Cottage, Orchard Terrace, Acomb,
Hexham, Northumberland
Italian Motorcycle Owners Club,
c/o Rosie Marston, 14 Rufford Close,
Barton Seagrave, Kettering
Jawa-CZ Owners MCC,
c/o Peter Edwards, 2 Churchill Close,
Breaston, Derbyshire
Kawasaki Owners Club, c/o John
Dalton, 37 Hinton Road, Runcorn
Laverda Owners Club,
c/o Dick Hutton, 78 Rufford Rise,
Sothall, Sheffield
Le Velocette Club, 32 Mackie
Avenue, Filton, Bristol, Avon
L E Velo Club, c/o Peter Greaves,
8 Heath Close, Walsall, West Midlands
Maico Owners Club,
c/o Phil Hingston, No Elms, Goosey,
Nr Faringdon, Oxon
Military Vehicle Trust, PO Box 6,
Fleet, Hants GU13 9PE
Morini Owners Club, c/o Richard
Laughton, 20 Fairford Close, Church
Hill, Redditch, Worcs
Morini Riders Club, 3 Minden Close,
Wokingham, Berkshire
Tel: 01734 793362
Moto Guzzi Club GB,
c/o Jenny Trengove, 53 Torbay Road,
Harrow, Middlesex
MV Agusta Club GB,
c/o Martyn Simpkins, 31 Baker Street,
Stapenhill, Burton-on-Trent
MZ Riders Club (South West),
c/o Alex Pearce, 80 Kingskirswell
Road, Newton Abbott, Devon
Tel: 01626 331584
**National Autocycle & Cyclemotor
Club,** c/o D Butler, 20 Bromford Hill,
Handsworth Wood, Birmingham
National Hill Climb Association,
43 Tyler Close, Hanham, Bristol
Tel: 0117 944 3569
New Imperial Owners Association,
c/o Mike Slater,
3 Fairview Drive, Higham, Kent
**North Devon British Motorcycle
Owners Club,** Bassett Lodge,
Pollards Hill, Torrington, North Devon
Norton Owners Club, c/o Dave
Fenner, Beeches, Durley Brook Road,
Durley, Southampton

**North Wilts British Motorcycle
Club,** 20 St Philips Road,
Stratton St Margaret, Swindon, Wilts
Norton Owners Club, 47 Pendennis
Park, Brislington, Bristol
Tel: 0117 977 2985
Panther Owners Club,
c/o A & J Jones, Coopers Cottage,
Park Lane, Castle Camps, Cambridge
**Raleigh Safety Seven and Early
Reliant Owners Club,**
26 Victoria Road, Southwick,
Sussex
Rickman Owners Club,
c/o Michael Foulds, 35 Otterbourne
Road, Chingford, London E4
Riders for Health, The Old Vicarage,
Norton, Nr. Daventry, Northampton
Royal Enfield Owners Club,
c/o John Cherry, Meadow Lodge Farm,
Henfield, Coalpit, Heath, Bristol
Rudge Enthusiasts Club,
c/o Sue Jackson-Scott, 117 Church
Lane, Chessington, Surrey
Scott Owners Club, c/o H Beal,
2 Whiteshott, Basildon, Essex
Shrivenham Motorcycle Club,
12-14 Townsend Road, Shrivenham,
Swindon, Wilts
Street Specials Motorcycle Club,
c/o E Warrington, 8 The Gallops,
Norton, Malton, North Yorkshire
Sunbeam Owners Club,
c/o Stewart Engineering, Church
Terrace, Harbury, Leamington Spa,
Warwickshire
Sunbeam Owners Fellowship,
PO Box 7, Market Harborough,
Leicestershire
Suzuki Owners Club,
c/o Ken Fulton, Wentworth Crescent,
Hayes, Middlesex
The Sidecar Register,
c/o John Proctor, 112 Briarlyn Road,
Birchencliffe, Huddersfield
**Trident and Rocket Three Owners
Club,** 63 Dunbar Road, Southport,
Merseyside
Triumph Motorcycle Club,
6 Hortham Lane, Almondsbury,
Bristol, Avon
Triumph Owners Club,
c/o Mrs M Mellish, 4 Douglas Avenue,
Harold Wood, Romford, Essex
Velocette Owners Club,
c/o Vic Blackman, 1 Mayfair,
Tilehurst, Reading, Berks
Vincent Owners Club,
9 Whitworth Close, Gosport,
Hampshire
Vintage Japanese MCC,
c/o John Dalton, 1 Maple Avenue,
Burchill, Onchan, Isle of Man
Vintage Motor Cycle Club,
Allen House, Wetmore Road,
Burton-on-Trent, Staffordshire
Tel: 01283 540557
Vintage Motorcycle Club of Ulster,
c/o Mrs M Burns, 20 Coach Road,
Comber, Newtownards, Co Down
Vintage Motor Scooter Club,
c/o Ian Harrop, 11 Ivanhoe Avenue,
Lowton St Lukes, Nr Warrington,
Cheshire
**Vintage Japanese Motorcycle
Club,** 9 Somerset Crescent,
Melksham, Wilts
Tel: 01225 702816
ZI Owners Club, c/o Sam Holt,
54 Hawhome Close, Congleton,
Cheshire

AJS & Matchless. The Postwar Models. Bacon. Covers the lightweight & heavyweight singles & twins from 1945. Marque history plus data on models. 191 pgs, 179 b&w ill. £14.95

Illustrated AJS & Matchless Buyers Guide. Redman. Detailed & fully illustrated review of all models. 160 pgs, 180 b&w ill..................................£10.95

Matchless & AJS Restoration. Bacon. Comprehensive guide to restoration, renovation & development history of all post-war production motorcycles. 304 pgs, 250 photos....................................£19.99

Illustrated BMW Buyers Guide. Knittel & Slabon. Covers every BMW model from 1923 to current models. 160 pgs, 150 b&w photos.................................£10.95

Classic Motorcycles. BMW. Morley & Woollett. All the favourite and most important BMWs in superb colour photography. 128 pgs, 120 colour ill. £10.99

BSA, The Complete Story. Wright. Detailed history of the marque & its models. Photographs & line drawings. Specification table. 160 pgs, 190 b&w ill.................£15.99

Illustrated BSA Buyers Guide. Bacon. Model by model analysis of the postwar singles, twins, triples & specials. 160 pgs, 200 ill. £10.95

Classic Motorcycles. BSA. Morley. All colour photographs of many BSA models. 128 pgs, 120 colour ill.........................£10.99

BSA Gold Star & Other Singles. Bacon. Covers the Gold Star; B,M,C ranges; Bantam & unit singles. 192 pgs, 161 ill. £14.95

The Gold Star Book. BMS. A workshop manual with parts list. 138 pgs, 174 ill........ ....£10.95

BSA Singles Restoration. Bacon. Covers all postwar pre-unit singles including the Gold Star, B, M, & C series plus four strokes & Bantams. 304 pgs, 250 ill...............£19.99

BSA Twin Restoration. Bacon. The essential restoration & renovation guide for all post-war twins. 240 pgs, 270 ill....£19.99

Classic Motorcycles. Walker. Covers country by country, over 150 of the world's finest bikes since 1945. Stunning colour photographs. Large format book. 110 pgs. £8.99

Ducati Tuning. Eke. For all the V-Twins with bevel drive camshafts. 112 pgs, 77 ill. £12.00

Ducati Singles Restoration. Walker. Diagrams, expert text, special techniques & guide to authentic Ducati detailing. 240 pgs, 250 ill. £18.99

Ducati Twins Restoration. Walker. A must for any Ducati twin owner or restorer. 240 pgs, 250 ill. £19.99

Big Book of Harley. Bolfert. The official publication of Harley-Davidson Inc. Traces the history of the company with over 1000 colour photos. 272 pgs, 1200 b&w & colour ill. £35.50

The Classic Harley. Williams. The bikes, their riders & their lifestyles in colour. Superb photos throughout. 144 pgs...**£16.99**

Illustrated Harley-Davidson Buyers Guide. Girdler. Second Ed. Details the models from 1936 to the new 1993 models. 176 pgs, 141 b&w ill. **£10.95**

Harley-Davidson Sportster Performance Handbook. Buzzelli. Complete guide to improving your Sportster. Traces the evolution of the Sportster from 1957 to today. 192 pgs, 300 b&w ill...............**£13.95**

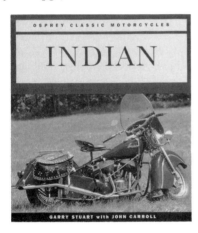

Tech Tips & Tricks. Vols 1 2 & 3. How to do it tips. Guides, charts & Harley-Davidson reference material.
Vol 1 ....**£8.95**
Vol 2 ....**£9.95**
Vol 3 ....**£8.95**

Honda. The Complete Story. Parker. Traces the company's development through all the major models from 1946 to the superbikes of the 80's & 90's. 160 pgs, 100 ill. **£14.99**

H.R.D. Motorcycles. Preece. The story of the marque, existing machines and their owners plus a spare parts list. 237 pgs, b&w photos...**£20.00**

Classic Motorcycles. Honda. Walker. A history in full colour. 128 pgs. **£10.99**

Indian Motorcycles. Kanter. The Indian's history from the early singles & twins to the age of the Scouts, Chiefs, Fours & the classic racers to the end of the line in 1953. 96 pgs, 80 colour photos....................................**£9.95**

Classic Motorcycles. Indian. Stuart & Carroll. A history in full colour. 128 pgs. ....
....**£10.99**

Indian Motorcycle Photographic History. Hatfield. From the first bicycle-derived 'motorcycles' of 1901 to the famous Chiefs, Scouts and Fours and the close in the 1960s. 239 pgs. b&w & colour............**£19.95**

Phil Irving. Irving. Phil Irving M.B.E., whose 60 year international career included the design of motorcycles, in particular the Vincent, motor cars & the famous Repco-Brabham Grand Prix engine, tells the fascinating story of his career in innovative auto design. 569 pgs. **£35.95**

Kawasaki-Sunrise to Z1. Bacon. All singles, twins & triples plus the 900 fours-1962 to 1976. 190pgs, b&w photos. ...**£14.95**

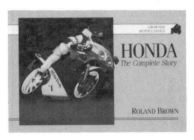

A Man Called Mike. Hilton. A biography of the legendary Mike Hailwood. 256 pgs, b&w & col. photos................................**£16.95**

Moto Guzzi (English Ed.) Colombo. Encyclopaedia of Moto Guzzi. The history, technical developments, catalogue of models, specifications and photos. 411 pgs, 552 b&w, 32 colour ill. **£44.95**

M V Agusta. Colombo & Patrignani. A history of the marque with a complete catalogue of production & racing models. English text. 245 pgs, 353 b&w, 20 colour ill.
....**£44.95**

Norton Illustrated Buyers Guide. Bacon. Information, specifications & technical details on all the models for the enthusiast, owner or potential buyer. 160 pgs, 150 ill. ...
....**£10.95**

Norton. Woollett. Follows the development of all Norton motorcycles, racing, off-road & Roadster. A definitive history of the oldest marque in the world. 320 pgs, 250 ill. ....
....**£25.00**

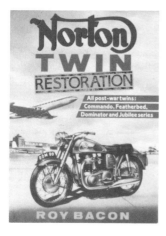

Norton Service & Overhaul Manual.
Neill. Covers the single cylinder 347cc 50,
490cc ES2 & the twin cylinder 250cc Jubilee,
350cc Navigator, 400cc Electra, 497cc 88, 88
de luxe 88SS, 99 Standard, 99SS, 99 de luxe,
650 Standard, 650 de luxe, 650 America,
650SS, 650 Manxman, 750 Atlas, 750
Scrambler, 750 G15 CS. 176 pgs, 123 ill. .....
....**£10.00**

Norton Twin Restoration. Bacon. Guide
to the renovation, restoration & development
history of all postwar Norton Twins
including Commando, Featherbed,
Dominator & Jubilee series. 240 pgs, 250 ill.
....**£19.99**

Royal Enfield. The Postwar Models.
Bacon. The 125, 150, 250, 350, 500, 700, 750
Singles & Twins. Analysis & specifications.
....**£14.95**

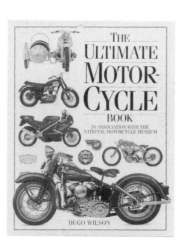

Rumi. Crippa. A model by model history of
the bikes. Competition history,
specifications & much more. Italian text.
255 pgs, 292 b&w, 16 colour ill. **£44.95**

Scott Motor Cycle: Yowling Two-Stroke.
Clew. The man, the machines, the factory:
it's successes and failures, racing results.
239 pgs. **£10.95**

Classic Motorcycles: Suzuki. Walker.
Full colour. A history from 1952 to the
multi-cylinder models including the liquid-
cooled 750's & the RE5. 128 pgs, full colour.
....**£10.99**

Triumph: The Complete Story. Davies.
From the days of Siegfried Bettmann in 1885
to the relaunch of the Triumph name in
1990. 160 pgs, 100 b&w ill. **£14.99**

**Classic Motorcycles. Triumph
Bonneville.** Bird. Complete history in full
colour. 128 pgs. **£10.99**

Triumph Tuning. Shenton. For the 500 &
650cc twin-cylinder engine and the 750cc
three. 54 pgs, b&w ill. **£6.00**

Triumph Singles. Bacon. Late pre-war
models incl. Terrier Cub, Trophy, Blazer &
scooters. A history plus specs., colours &
recognition. 127 pgs, 71 b&w photos, 3 ill....
....**£13.95**

Triumph Twin Restoration. Bacon.
Comprehenisve restoration guide. 240 pgs,
250 ill. **£19.99**

The Velocette Saga. Allen. The story of
the Velocette firm & the designers &
engineers who worked for it, & above all the
motorcycle they produced. 229 pgs, b&w
photos...**£19.99**

Velocette: Viper/Venom/Thruxton. 350
Singles. BMS. Service manual. 64 pgs, 134
ill...**£8.95**

Vespa: An Illustrated History. Brockway.
Fascinating collection of photographs. 96
pgs, b&w photos...................................**£9.99**

Villiers: Singles & Twins. Bacon. Covers
the Villiers powered motorcycle & all British
powered 'look alikes'. 188 pgs, b&w ill. ....
....**£14.95**

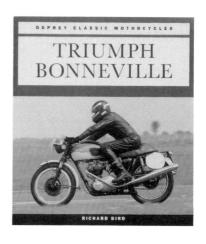

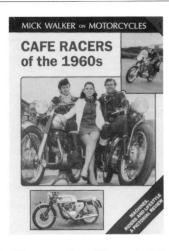

Classic Motorcycles. Vincent. Wherrett. Complete history in full colour. 128 pgs. **£10.99**

Know Thy Beast. Stevens. Comprehensive information on restoration & maintenance of postwar Vincent motorcycles. 259 pgs, 24 ill. **£19.95**

The Ultimate Motorcycle Book. Wilson. Chronicles the development of the motorcycle from 1885. More than 200 classic & contemporary bikes featured & shows exactly how a bike works with step-by-step diagrams explaining the principles behind the mechanics. 192 pgs, 650 colour ill. **£15.99**

A Twist of the Wrist. Vol. 1. Code. The motorcycle racer's handbook. A step-by-step manual explaining how to successfully ride, race & improve riding skills. 117 pgs, 73 ill. **£13.95**

A Twist of the Wrist. Vol. 2. Code. Uncovers & traces, action-by-action, the direct links between man & machine. 117 pgs, b&w ill. **£15.99**

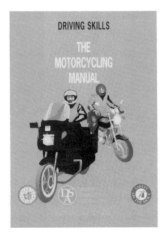

Driving Skills. The Motorcycle Manual. H.M.S.O. Compiled by the Driving Standards Agency to promote road safety through better riding standards. Full colour pages packed with information. 152 pgs. **£7.50**

Café Racers of the 1960s. Walker. A pictorial review of the machines, riders & lifestyle. 93 pgs, b&w ill. **£9.95**

Motorcycle Basics Manual. Haynes. 164 pgs, 394 ill. **£10.63**

Motorcycle Electrical Manual. Haynes. 2nd edition. 125 pgs. **£10.63**

Motorcycle Carburettor Manual, Haynes. app. 100 pgs. **£10.63**

Motorcycle Workshop Practice Manual. Haynes. App. 128 pgs. **£10.63**

Motorcycle Restorer's Workshop Companion. Purnell. The complete guide to techniques & tools for bike restoration & repairs. 160 pgs, 150 b&w ill. **£12.99**

Tuning for Speed. Irving. 6th Ed. How to increase the performance of motorcycle engines for touring, racing & competition. 265 pgs. **£24.95**

Workshop Manuals: Haynes & Clymer manuals for many modern bikes. Reprints of original manuals for some classic British bikes.

VIDEOS:

Castrol History of Motorcycle Racing. Vol 1. How it all began and the TT. 60 mins **£10.99**

Castrol History of Motorcycle Racing. Vol 2. Birth of the GP & the Japanese arrival. 72 mins. **£10.99**

Castrol History of Motorcycle Racing. Vol 3. The other champions & pressure, money & the need to win. 60 mins. ..**£10.99**

Harley Magic. The bike, the legend, the lifestyle. 55 mins. **£10.99**

Tribute to Bob McIntyre. The Northwest 200, 1958. The Right Line 1960. 40 mins.... ....**£17.99**

Heavy Duty. 90 Years with America's bike. 70 mins...**£12.99**

From the Jaws of Victory. The story of the British motorcycle industry. 55 mins..... ....**£14.99**

Vespa Story. If you ever owned a Vespa, this video will bring a lump to your throat... 30 mins...**£14.99**

DIRECTORY OF MUSEUMS

The National Motorcycle Museum:
Coventry Road, Solihull, West Midlands.
Tel: 0121-704 2784.

The National Motorcycle Museum, opened in 1984, was established as a permanent tribute to Norton encompassing the whole of the British Motorcycle industry. The museum occupies 3.4 hectares in rural surroundings, displaying 650 machines, 95% of which are owned by the museum, with the remainder being on loan from collections and private owners across the world.

Potential acquisitions are researched, investigated and 'handled' by the Museum's worldwide network of agents and contacts. Restoration work is then carried out by enthusiasts throughout the country, all of them painstakingly precise in the mechanics, engineering requirements and historical accuracy of each machine they work on. A great many of them work in private workshops for the Museum as a 'labour of love', and they are all, in some way, veterans of the British motorcycle industry.

The museum features a fully licensed restaurant, a souvenir shop full of motorcycling memorabilia as well as free car parking.

Open every day from 10am-6pm.
Take Junction 6 off the M42 and the A45, opposite the National Exhibition Centre. Birmingham International Airport and Railway are minutes away and the No. 900 bus from Birmingham City centre stops right outside.

Sammy Miller Museum,
Gore Road, New Milton, Hants.
Tel: 01425 619696

Sammy Miller is a living legend in the world of motorcycle racing, and what started out as a hobby 30 years ago has become a collection of what is arguably the best selection of competition motorcycles in the country. The museum was opened in 1983 by John Surtees and is much more than a static collection. All bikes are in working order and wherever possible are run in classic bike events throughout the year. Many of the racing bikes are still fully competitive.

At present there are 200 bikes in the Museum, many of them extremely rare. New exhibits are being sought all the time to add to the collection, with much of the restoration work being carried out on the premises by Sammy Miller himself. There are interesting artefacts and items of memorabilia connected to the motorcycling world on display, including many cups and trophies won by Sammy over the years. A typical motorcycle workshop of 1925 has been reconstructed, showing a large display of the tools used at that time.

Sammy Miller's road-racing ability confirmed his all-round talent, and brought him a ride on importer Terry Hill's 250 Sportmax NSU. He is seen here at Lurgan in April 1956.

Open 10.30am-4.30pm every day, April-October
10.30am-4.30pm Sats and Suns, November-March
The museum is situated 15 miles west of Southampton and 10 miles east of Bournemouth at New Milton, Hants.

Battlesbridge Motorcycle Museum:
Battlesbridge Antiques Centre, Maltings Road,
Battlesbridge, Essex. Tel: 01268 769392.
40 classic machines in a small informal 'museum'.
Open Sundays 10am-1pm.
Adults £1, children free.

Birmingham Museum of Science & Industry:
Newhall Street, Birmingham. Tel: 0121-235 1651.
A small collection of motorcycles right in the heart
of the city.
Open Monday to Saturday 9.30am-5pm.
Sunday 2pm-5pm. Closed December 25-26, and
January 1. Admission free.

Bristol Industrial Museum: Princes Wharf,
City Docks, Bristol. Tel: 0117 925 1470.
A small collection of Bristol-made Douglas
machines, including the only surviving V4 of 1908.
There is also a 1972 Quasar.
Open Saturday to Wednesday 10am-1pm and
2pm-5pm. Closed Thursdays and Fridays, also
Good Friday, December 25-27 and January 1.
Adults £2, under 16s free.

Brooklands Museum:
The Clubhouse, Brooklands Road, Weybridge,
Surrey. Tel: 01932 857381.
The birthplace of British motorsport and aviation,
Brooklands has several motorcycles on display.
Open Saturday and Sunday 10am-4pm. Guided
tours at 10.30am and 2pm on Tuesdays,
Wednesdays and Thursdays. Adults £4, OAPs and
students £3, children £2.

Foulkes-Halbard of Filching
Filching Manor, Jevington Road, Wannock,
Polegate, Sussex. Tel: 01323 487838
A collection of 30 motorcycles, including pre-'40s
American bikes ex-Steve McQueen, as well as 100
cars dating from 1893-1993.
Open 7 days a week in summer 10.30-4.30pm.
Thurs-Sunday in winter, or by appointment
Adults £3, OAPs and children £2.

Grampian Transport Museum:
Alford, Aberdeenshire, Scotland. Tel: 019755 62292.
A collection of 30-40 machines ranging from a 1902
Beeston Humber to a Norton F1. Mods and
Rockers caff display with Triton and Triumph
Tina scooter. Competition section includes 1913
Indian twin and 1976 Rob North replica
Trident racer.
Open March 28-October 31, 10am-5pm. Adults
£2.30, children 80p, OAPs £1.50, family ticket £5.

Haynes Sparkford Motor Museum:
Sparkford, Yeovil, Somerset. Tel: 01963 40804.
Collection of 28 machines from a 1914 BSA
onwards. Video theatre. Bookshop.
Open Monday to Sunday 9.30am-5.30pm. Closed
December 25-26 and January 1. Adults £3.50,
OAPs £3, children £2.20.

Midland Motor Museum:
Stourbridge Road, Bridgnorth, Shropshire.
Tel: 01746 761761.
Owned by Morris, the oil company, this collection
includes 50 motorcycles.
Open every day in July, August and September
10.30am-5pm, and Saturdays, Sundays and Bank
Holidays 11am-4pm. Adults £3.50, OAPs £2.80,
children 5-16 £1.75, family ticket £9.95.

Murray's Motorcycle Museum:
Bungalow Corner, TT Course, Isle of Man.
Tel: 01624 861719.
Collection of 140 machines, including Hailwood's
250cc Mondial racer and the amazing 500cc
4 cylinder roadster designed by John Wooler.
Open May to September 10am-5pm. Adults £2,
OAPs and children £1.

Museum of British Road Transport:
St. Agnes Lane, Hales Street, Coventry.
Tel: 01203 832425.
Collection includes 65 motorcycles, with local firms
such as Coventry Eagle, Coventry Victor, Francis-
Barnett, Triumph and Rudge well represented.
Close to city centre.
Open every day except December 24-26,
10am-5pm. Adults £2.50, children, OAPs and
unemployed £1.50.

Museum of Transport:
Kelvin Hall, 1 Bunhouse Road, Glasgow.
Tel: 0141-357 3929.
Small collection of motorcycles includes
Automobile Association BSA combination.
Open Monday to Saturday 10am-5pm. Sunday
11am-5pm. Closed December 25 and January 1.
Admission free.

The Myreton Motor Museum:
Aberlady, East Lothian, Scotland.
Tel: 018757 288.
Small collection of motorcycles includes 1926 350cc
Chater-Lea racer and Egli Vincent.
Open Easter to October 10am-5pm and October to
Easter 10am-6pm. Closed December 25 and
January 1. Adults £2, children 50p.

The National Motor Museum:
Beaulieu, Hants. Tel: 01590 612123/612345.
Important motorcycle collection.
Reference and photographic libraries.
Open Easter to September 10am-6pm, October to
Easter 10am-5pm. Closed December 25.
Adults £6.75, OAPs/students £5.25, children £4.75
(includes Museum, rides and drives, Monastic
Life Exhibition and entry to Palace House and
grounds).

Royal Museum of Scotland:
Chambers Street, Edinburgh, Scotland.
Tel: 0131-225 7534.
Small display of engines and complete machines
includes the world's first 4 cylinder motorcycle, an
1895 Holden.
Open Monday to Saturday 10am-5pm. Sunday
2pm-5pm. Closed December 25, January 1.
Admission free.

The Science Museum:
Exhibition Road, South Kensington, London SW7.
Tel: 0171-589 3456.
Interesting collection of engines and complete
machines, including cutaway BSA A10 and
Yamaha XS1100. Recent additions to displays
include 1940 500cc BMW and 1969 Honda CB750.
Open Monday to Saturday 10am-6pm. Sunday
11am-6pm. Closed December 24-26. Adults £4,
OAPs and children £2.10, disabled free.

The bulk of the Science Museum's motorcycle
collection is stored at **Wroughton Airfield** near
Swindon, Wilts. Tel: 0793 814466.

Stanford Hall Motorcycle Museum:
Stanford Hall, Lutterworth, Leics.
Tel: 01788 860250.
The collection of older machines and racers.
Open Saturdays, Sundays, Bank Holiday Mondays
and following Tuesdays Easter to September,
2.30pm-6pm. (12 noon-6pm when a special event
is taking place.)
Admission to grounds: Adults £1.60, children 70p.
Motorcycle Museum: Adults 90p, children 20p.

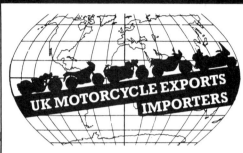

146